D0845042

THE KINGS & QUEENS OF BRITAIN

The Kings & Queens of Britain

Cath Senker

This edition published in 2019 by Sirius Publishing, a division of
Arcturus Publishing Limited,
26/27 Bickels Yard, 151–153 Bermondsey Street,
London SE1 3HA

ISBN: 978-1-78950-571-9
AD006864UK

Printed in China

Contents

Introduction: The Impact of the Monarchy ... 6

Chapter 1 Saxons and Danes – 800s to 1066 ... 8

Chapter 2 The Normans – 1066 to 1154 ... 22

Chapter 3 The Struggle for Power in Wales – 800 to 1536 ... 34

Chapter 4 The House of Anjou – 1154 to 1272 ... 42

Chapter 5 Scotland: From the Viking Invasions to Independence – 800 to 1424 ... 56

Chapter 6 The Plantagenets – 1272 to 1399 ... 66

Chapter 7 The Houses of Lancaster and York – 1399 to 1485 ... 80

Chapter 8 The Tudors – 1485 to 1603 ... 94

Chapter 9 Renaissance Scotland – 1424 to 1625 ... 122

Chapter 10 The Stuarts – 1603 to 1714 ... 128

Chapter 11 The House of Hanover – 1714 to 1901 ... 148

Chapter 12 The Houses of Saxe-Coburg, Gotha and Windsor – 1901 to present day ... 172

Chapter notes ... 188

Index ... 190

Picture Credits ... 192

THE IMPACT OF THE MONARCHY

On 18 May 2018, Prince Harry, grandson of Queen Elizabeth II, walked down the aisle with Meghan Markle. Their royal wedding was celebrated in exuberant style, with a rousing sermon, a 20-strong gospel choir singing 'Stand by Me' and a cello performance by the first black musician to win the title 'Young Musician of the Year'. Meghan was no typical royal bride and this was no traditional wedding – yet it indicated the extraordinary adaptability of the British monarchy, which first emerged in Anglo-Saxon times and has endured to the present day.

The monarchy arose alongside other social changes. Around 600, a feudal structure began to develop, with lords owning private land that was worked by serfs; clear social divisions were established between the landed and landless.

At the same time, the power of the central state was growing, owing to the military conquest of territory. The king gained significance as the most important feudal lord and as a war leader, and from the time of Athelstan (925–939), monarchs ruled all of England. Early kings had a huge political impact on the country, and their personality was key to the success or failure of their reign. The coronation of a new monarch was a decisive event; the sovereign would probably rule for life, and some remained at the helm for decades. Political life was quite different to the cycle of regular elections we experience in modern times.

Left: *The Imperial State Crown is presented to Queen Elizabeth II before the state opening of Parliament. The Crown Jewels are held in the Tower of London.*

Throughout history, the actions of individual monarchs have affected social, political and economic affairs. Strong rulers have conquered and subjugated territory, including William I in England, Edward I in Wales and Robert the Bruce in Scotland. Their impact has sometimes been unintentional; developments have occurred as by-products of policies. Social change was triggered by Henry VIII's personal imperative for a divorce, which led to the separation of the English Church from the Catholic Church, the Reformation and the establishment of Protestantism as the state religion. In the 17th century, Charles I's inability to compromise with Parliament caused political conflict that contributed to the English Civil War and the Interregnum. After the restoration of the monarchy, Parliament substantially increased its powers.

The monarch's need for tax revenues to pay for the royal court and prosecute wars led to economic changes. Taxes were imposed initially on land, and the landowning barons who were encumbered by this taxation became determined to protect their own interests and exert some control over Crown expenditure. Over time, from the *Magna Carta* onwards (1215), the power of the monarchy to manage spending was gradually transferred to Parliament. From the 18th century, economic power began to shift away from the landowners who sat in the House of Lords towards the businesspeople and industrialists who occupied the House of Commons; as the latter gained ascendance, the Commons became the more powerful house in Parliament.

During the 18th and 19th centuries, constitutional monarchy developed – the institution lost its executive role and adopted an advisory role in government. As the autocratic monarchies of Europe fell away in the early 20th century, the British monarchy preserved itself by carving out a ceremonial niche and becoming a focus for national identity that was cemented during two world wars. This book tells the story of a remarkably resilient institution.

CHAPTER I

SAXONS AND DANES
800s–1066

From the 5th to the 7th centuries, Angles, Saxons and Jutes from northern Germany established kingdoms in England. Traditionally, historians perceived their invasion as a violent takeover, but recently opinions have shifted. Although the native British people offered some resistance, many historians now see it as a less forceful conquest, marked by social integration and intermarriage with the local population. By 700, twelve main Anglo-Saxon kingdoms had formed and they fought among themselves for supremacy. It was not until the 10th century that England came under one ruler. Once in control, the Anglo-Saxon monarchs created administrative systems and laws to govern the land. In the 900s, Danish invaders persistently attacked England, raiding year after year; they finally seized the English throne the following century. In turn, their dominance was challenged by growing Norman influence.

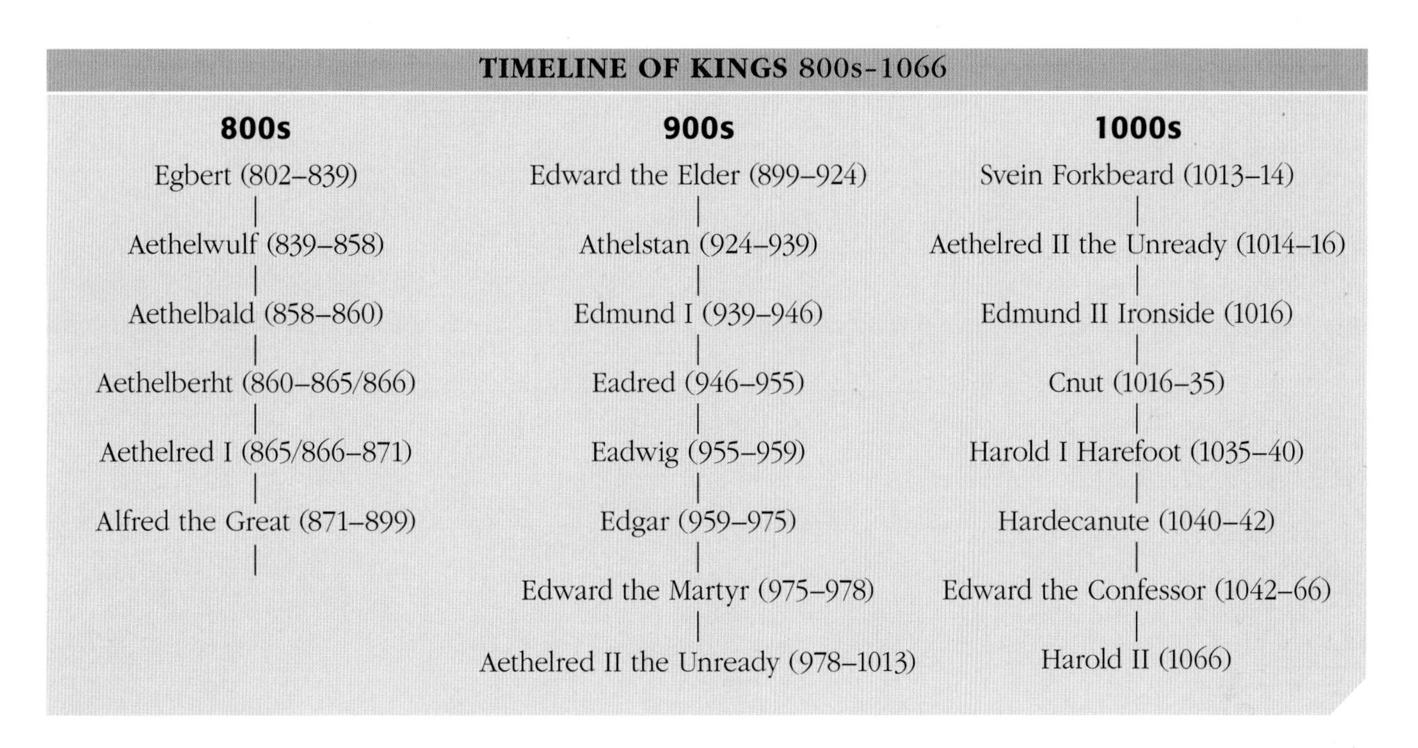

TIMELINE OF KINGS 800s-1066

800s	900s	1000s
Egbert (802–839)	Edward the Elder (899–924)	Svein Forkbeard (1013–14)
Aethelwulf (839–858)	Athelstan (924–939)	Aethelred II the Unready (1014–16)
Aethelbald (858–860)	Edmund I (939–946)	Edmund II Ironside (1016)
Aethelberht (860–865/866)	Eadred (946–955)	Cnut (1016–35)
Aethelred I (865/866–871)	Eadwig (955–959)	Harold I Harefoot (1035–40)
Alfred the Great (871–899)	Edgar (959–975)	Hardecanute (1040–42)
	Edward the Martyr (975–978)	Edward the Confessor (1042–66)
	Aethelred II the Unready (978–1013)	Harold II (1066)

Below: *This Anglo-Saxon manuscript from the early-11th century shows labourers ploughing a field.*

ALFRED THE GREAT (871–899)

The youngest of at least six children of an aristocratic family, Alfred emerged to become a powerful monarch and the best known of the Anglo-Saxon kings. The only English monarch known as 'the great', he mounted a fierce defence against the Danish invaders, constructed fortified towns and extensively revised Anglo-Saxon law. Alfred made steps towards the Crown's control of England, and by the 890s, his charters and coins referred to him as 'king of the English'. He is often considered the first king of England, although he ruled only part of the country.

Below: *The statue of Alfred the Great in Winchester. Winchester was the capital of the kingdom of Wessex.*

THE DANES – DESTRUCTIVE AND CONSTRUCTIVE

Below: *A Viking axe blade, c. AD 1000*

England was attractive to the Vikings of Denmark, for its fertile farmland and the riches of its monasteries – and their longboats allowed them to reach its shores. Alfred's reign was dominated by struggles with the Danes to control England. In 871, Alfred defeated Danish forces at the Battle of Ashdown, in Berkshire, but they continued to launch attacks in Wessex. Following Alfred's victory in 878 at the Battle of Edington, near Trowbridge in Wiltshire, they made peace. The Danish raids had been hugely destructive – they razed settlements and stole booty. Yet they brought advances too. The Danes introduced the axe, which was probably used for clearing forests, allowing the expansion of agriculture. They brought their sophisticated sailing technology and navigation techniques, using a sun compass to check the position of the sun, and skilful craftsmanship, making beads from melted coloured glass and elegant combs from animal bones.

ALFRED BURNS THE CAKES

As author Rudyard Kipling once commented, 'If history were taught in the form of stories, it would never be forgotten.' Many people know of King Alfred from the tale of his poor baking skills. In January 878, the Vikings invaded Alfred's base in Chippenham, and his forces were routed. The king and his men scattered around the Somerset Levels, relying on food and shelter from the locals. Alfred had taken refuge with a peasant woman, who asked him to keep an eye on her cakes baking by the fire. Consumed by his worries, he allowed the cakes to burn and was scolded by his hostess. Alfred subsequently regrouped his forces in Athelney – a tiny low-lying village in the marshes, surrounded by reeds, woods and scrubland – where he planned the retaliatory assault against the Vikings in Edington.

SECURING THE KINGDOM

Once in control, King Alfred reorganized his army and introduced a military levy system. At any one time, half the militia were active, while the other half remained in reserve. To fight the Danes at sea, he built a naval fleet with superior ships: 'full nigh twice as long as the others; some had sixty oars, and some had more; they were both swifter and steadier, and also higher than the others'.[1] In 884, Alfred sent a fleet against the Danes of East Anglia and he took London in 886. He realized he could not drive the Danes out of the whole country, so he made a partition treaty. England was divided – the north and east between the Rivers Thames and Tees became Danish territory, while Alfred controlled London, West Mercia and Kent. The main Danish settlements were Leicestershire, Lincolnshire, Nottinghamshire and Yorkshire; in the 11th century, the Danish area became known as the Danelaw.

Above: *A Viking helmet. The first Viking raid on the British Isles came at the monastery of Lindisfarne in 793.*

For defence, King Alfred constructed around 25 burghs – fortified centres across southern England, guarded by professional soldiers. The burghs allowed people to live in peace; they

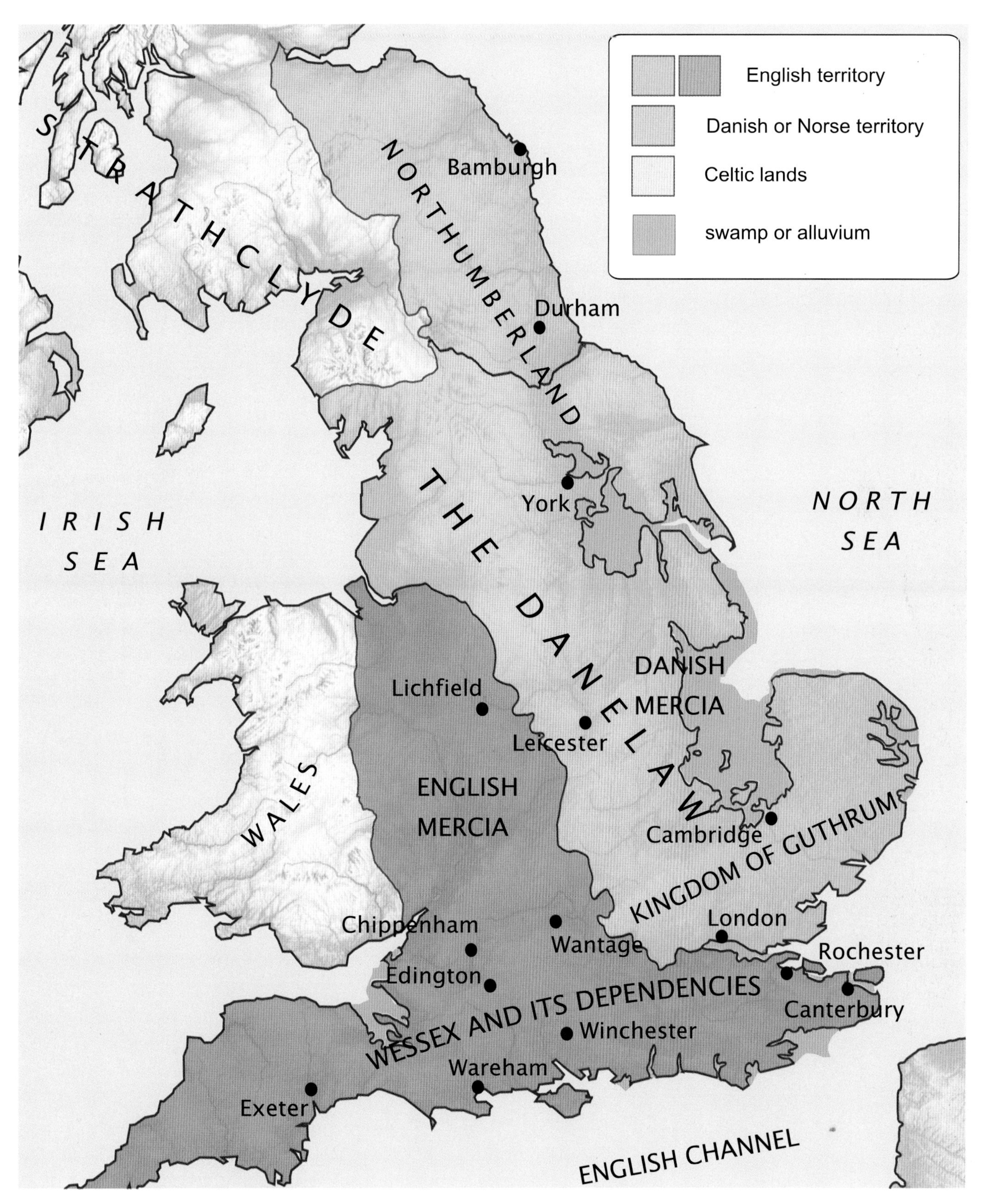

Above: *A map of England in 878. The country was split into the Anglo-Saxon kingdoms of Wessex, Mercia and Northumbria, and the Danelaw.*

developed into the medieval towns of the south, and the king encouraged the development of industries. The English were no longer purely rural folk.

RELIGION, EDUCATION AND LAW

King Alfred also turned his hand to the Church and education, restoring monasteries and convents that had been demolished in Viking raids. He introduced a school system for the sons of noblemen, believing that secular officials as well as churchmen should be educated. Alfred loved books, and was one of the few English monarchs to write books himself. He had 'books most necessary for all men to know' translated from Latin to English, and it is believed he commissioned the *Anglo-Saxon Chronicle* (see below).

The king established a legal code to form the body of Anglo-Saxon law. He explained his process:

> *I … collected these [laws] together and ordered to be written many of them which our forefathers observed, those which I liked; and many of those which I did not like I rejected with the advice of my councillors … For I dared not presume to set in writing at all many of my own, because it was unknown to me what would please those who should come after us …*[2]

The Anglo-Saxons had a council of important nobles and bishops called the Witan, which they could call upon for advice. Alfred clearly accepted that it was necessary to seek advice from his councillors, one of the marks of a successful ruler. By consolidating his territory and developing the legal system, Alfred facilitated the extension of control over the whole of England by his successors.

BOROUGHS

Alfred rebuilt London, which the Danish raids had made almost uninhabitable, renovating the walls of the old Roman city of Londinium, and restoring the waterfront. He offered settlers plots of land called burghs, which they would defend in times of war. The burghs created in London in the 880s formed the basis of the city centre, between Cheapside and the Thames. The word 'borough' comes from 'burgh', meaning 'fortress'.

THE *ANGLO-SAXON CHRONICLE*

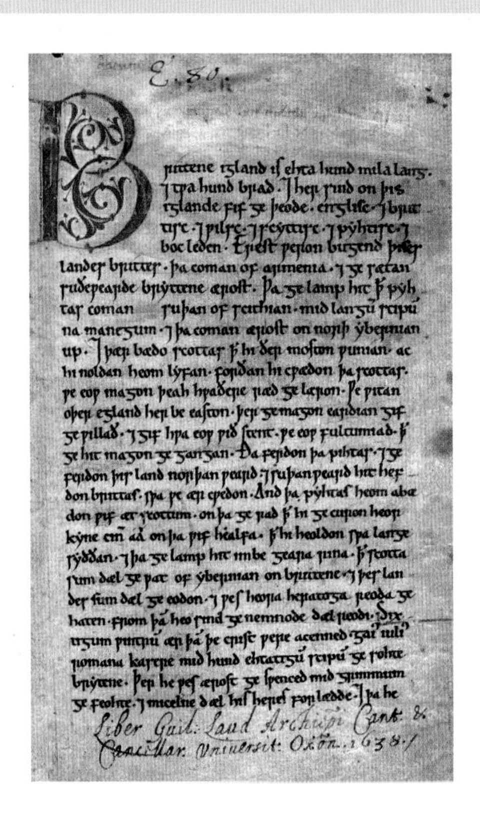

A main source for our knowledge of Anglo-Saxon and Norman England, the *Anglo-Saxon Chronicle* provides a narrative of historical events, covering the breadth of English life, from agriculture, trade and coinage to religion, laws and wars. Its coverage is patchy, with more information about some eras than others; you won't find much about King Cnut, but it is rich in detail for the hundred years from Edward the Confessor's reign. The chronicle has survived to this day, although one of the seven manuscripts was destroyed in a fire in 1731.

Above: *The opening page of the* Anglo-Saxon Chronicle.

EDWARD THE ELDER (899–924)

Above: *Edward the Elder, depicted in the* Genealogical roll of the kings of England, *c. 1307.*

Described by William of Malmesbury as 'much inferior to his father in the cultivation of letters' yet 'incomparably more glorious in the power of his rule,'[3] Alfred's eldest son Edward increased the territory of the English Crown and achieved the allegiance of the Danes, Scots and Britons (the indigenous pre-Anglo-Saxon people). His military success was in large part due to an alliance with his sister Aethelflaed. They recaptured a large area of land from the Danes, defeating them near Tettenhall, Northumbria, in 910. Edward extended his rule over most of England, except for the Kingdom of York, and subjected the Mercians to his rule. He also forced the submission of Constantine II of Scotland and the Kings of Strathclyde in 921 although it is unlikely he had direct control over Scotland. Edward laid the ground for the unification of England under his successor.

ANGLO-SAXON SOCIETY

By the 10th century, the laws defined the social hierarchy in England. At the bottom were slaves, frequently victims of misfortune who had been sold into servitude. Then there were the semi-free – cottagers tied to their lord. They were neither paid nor paid rent, but worked on the land, giving a proportion of its produce to the lord. Above them were the warriors and lords – the landowners. Owning land was the key to wealth. Interestingly, women in the Saxon era had more freedom than in later times. They could not be forced to marry and divorce was easy to obtain. High-ranked women could own land and property, and make wills. Ordinary women had a varied working life; they were responsible for housework and childcare, but also farmed and made clothes.

THE LADY OF THE MERCIANS

The 16-year-old daughter of Alfred the Great, Aethelflaed, was married in 886 to Aethelred, the ruler of Mercia. At this time, the eastern part of Mercia was held by the Vikings. Leading their army together, Aethelred and Aethelflaed took back large swathes of Mercia. When her husband grew sick, Aethelflaed led building projects and military campaigns; she campaigned alongside her brother Edward to defeat the Vikings in 910. After Aethelred died in 911, Aethelflaed became the sole ruler of Mercia as the Lady of the Mercians.

Left: *Aethelflaed, the daughter of Alfred the Great and ruler of Mercia, portrayed in the 13th-century* Cartulary and Customs of Abingdon Abbey. *She was the only female Anglo-Saxon ruler.*

Opposite: *Athelstan presents a book to St Cuthbert in Bede's* Life of Saint Cuthbert.

ATHELSTAN (924–39)

In his personal life, King Athelstan, son of Edward the Elder, was a devout man who loved collecting religious manuscripts and saints' relics, which he offered to churches and communities to gain their support. As king, he extended his authority over the whole of England, ending opposition in Cornwall. All five Welsh kings submitted to him, and he accepted their homage and a substantial annual tribute of gold, silver and 25,000 oxen. Athelstan also invaded Scotland – in 927, he defeated a combined army of Danes and Scots in York, forcing the King of Scotland and the northern kings to submit to him.

Determined to maintain control, Athelstan brought in legal codes to strengthen his grip over the kingdom. He continued to defend the realm with fortified burghs, controlling river access to deter Viking raiders. Now England was a larger kingdom, it became impossible to rule the whole country centrally, so Athelstan divided it into shires, areas often centred on King Alfred's burghs. He appointed shire-reeves, or sheriffs, to run the shires. Each shire was divided into hundreds, and every shire and hundred had its own court. The shires later became the counties we know today. The economic growth of the burghs continued, and they became important trading centres.

AETHELRED II, THE UNREADY (978–1016)

Aethelred II became king at the tender age of 12 after his half-brother King Edward the Martyr was murdered. As was common at the time, councillors ruled in his name and trained him for monarchy until he reached adulthood. Although he enjoyed a long reign and had some success in strengthening the state of England using the shire-reeve system, he earned his poor reputation because of Viking invasions and civil war in the final years of his reign.[4] Aethelred bought off the invaders to try to prevent them from attacking, but his policy met with little success.

THE CAPTURE OF AELFHEAH

After Canterbury was besieged, the Danes captured archbishop Aelfheah, a significant blow to the morale of their enemies. As described in the *Anglo-Saxon Chronicle*, Aelfheah:

> *... was then captive*
> *he who erewhile was*
> *head of the English race*
> *and Christendom.*
> *There might then be seen*
> *misery, where men oft*
> *erewhile saw bliss,*
> *in that hapless city ...*[5]

The Vikings demanded a ransom for Aelfheah's release, which was proferred; when they demanded a further amount, the archbishop ordered that it should not be paid. At a drunken feast, his captors felled him with an axe.

WHY 'THE UNREADY'

The name Aethelred (or Ethelred) means 'noble counsel'; his nickname comes from the Old English word 'unraed', meaning 'no counsel' or' ill advised' and is a pun on his real name. 'Unready', a later corruption of the term, implies that the king was at fault rather than being poorly counselled.

Left: *Aethelred the Unready, from the 12th-century* Abingdon Chronicle.

THE BATTLE OF MALDON, 991

Above: *A 20th-century illustration of the Battle of Maldon. The battle inspired a 325-line Old English poem of the same name.*

At Maldon in Essex, Ealdorman Byrhtnoth challenged the invaders to battle rather than bribing them to depart. He even permitted them to cross the causeway from Northey Island to engage in combat. Casualties were heavy on both sides, but when Byrhtnoth was killed, the Vikings gained the upper hand and achieved victory.

The *Anglo-Saxon Chronicle* described the onslaught: 'Olaf came with 93 ships to Folkestone, and ravaged round about it, and then from there he went to Sandwich, and so from there to Ipswich, and overran it all, and so to Maldon. And Ealdorman Byrhtnoth came against him there with his army and fought against him; and they killed the ealdorman there and had control of the field.'[6]

England was subjected to a torrent of Viking raids in the 980s and 990s, probably launched from the Isle of Man or from Viking colonies in Ireland. In 991, Olaf Tryggvason led a major incursion from Norway, seeking plunder to bolster his power back home. His fleet invaded every year for the following three years.

SUING FOR PEACE

Below: *A 13th-century manuscript shows the invasion of England by Svein Forkbeard.*

Rather than resisting, Aethelred decided to sue for peace. He paid off the Scandinavian attackers with the enormous sum of £16,000. Olaf accepted baptism and went home peacefully to Norway. But the generous bribe encouraged the Vikings to return for more rich pickings: further Norwegian invaders arrived in 997, 999, 1001 and 1002. Aethelred made a couple of attempts to fight back, but it would have taken vast resources to overcome them. In November 1002, the king ordered a massacre of Danes in England in an attempt to deter the raiders, but it had the opposite effect, leading to a retaliatory Danish invasion in 1003.

FORKBEARD

The King of Denmark, Svein Forkbeard, led the 1003 incursion, and he raided repeatedly over the following four years, causing widespread devastation in southern and eastern England. In 1007, a desperate Aethelred paid Svein £36,000 to go away. The king finally opted for defence, building a fleet of

TURNING BACK THE WAVES

According to legend, King Cnut was so powerful that he was able to turn back the waves in the sea. In reality, the story comes from King Cnut's rebuttal to his sycophantic courtiers. They would praise him, saying 'even the waves obey you.' To put a stop to such nonsense, he marched them down to the beach to prove that it was not true. The story was first recorded in the 12th century and is likely to be apocryphal, yet several places claim to the site of this event, including Thorney Island (an island on the Thames at Westminster), Southampton, Bosham in West Sussex and Gainsborough in Lincolnshire.

Above: *An illustration of King Cnut from a medieval manuscript. Cnut was king of Norway and Denmark as well as England, which combined to make the North Sea Empire.*

warships that assembled at Sandwich in 1009. No immediate threat materialized, so the king unwisely dispersed the fleet. As soon as he did so, the Danes, under Thorkell, launched further invasions. In September 1011, his army plundered the south-east, sacking Canterbury and later murdering the archbishop, Aelfheah. The following year, Svein Forkbeard succeeded in conquering England and bringing it under Danish rule. Yet when he died in 1014, his son Cnut was not accepted by the English Witan, and Aethelred regained control of the throne until his death in 1016.

CNUT (1016–35)

Cnut resolved to achieve his father's goal of ruling England. After King Aethelred died, Cnut battled Aethelred's son, Edmund Ironside, forcing him to partition the kingdom. One month later, Edmund was dead, and England was in Cnut's hands.

The Danish king consolidated his regime by brutally eliminating his enemies. He married Aethelred's widow, probably to prevent her sons from claiming the throne (she shrewdly smuggled them out of the country). Cnut exiled Edmund's younger brother Eadwig, and he was probably killed. To protect his kingdom, he formed a small standing army of housecarls – highly trained, professional soldiers.

After the violent beginning to his reign, Cnut focused on becoming acceptable to his English subjects. He maintained the English system of government, agreeing with the Witan to observe the existing laws. Cnut divided the country into four earldoms – Northumbria, Mercia, East Anglia and Wessex. He called his rulers earls rather than ealdormen but their job was more or less the same, and he mostly appointed Englishmen to the posts.

Cnut became a generous benefactor of the Church, becoming the patron of St Edmund's

Abbey in Bury; King Edmund had been shot to death by Cnut's ancestor Ivar the Boneless. He also had the relics of Aelfheah (see page 15) moved from London to Canterbury. Such actions helped reconcile the English to their Danish ruler.

EDWARD THE CONFESSOR (1042–66)

The only surviving son of Aethelred II (see page 15), and therefore the leading Anglo-Saxon claimant to the throne, Edward was sent away to Normandy for his safety aged 11. He remained in exile until he was invited back as heir to the throne after the reigns of Cnut's sons (1035–42). The first 11 years of Edward's reign were dominated by a power struggle with Godwine, Earl of Wessex. Edward introduced his Norman friends to the court, which led to resentment among the nobles of the powerful houses of Mercia and Wessex. But the remaining years were relatively peaceful, with England enjoying growing prosperity and a rising population.

While Edward preferred to make Norman connections through his mother Emma, daughter of the Duke of Normandy, the powerful Earl of Wessex favoured links with the Scandinavian countries. Edward gave Norman nobles important positions in government and brought French courtiers into the Church, offering them abbacies and other senior benefices. This made him unpopular with Godwine and his allies. In 1051, Edward signed a treaty of friendship with William of Normandy. Godwine was incensed and staged a revolt in the winter of 1051–52. He was defeated and driven into exile, but later that year he returned, and was joined by many of his former thanes (men who held land he had granted them). To avoid civil war, Edward agreed to restore Godwine's property and allow his family to regain their positions of power. After Godwine died the following year, his son Harold Godwinson headed the family.

WHO WAS EDWARD'S HEIR?

Since Edward's marriage was childless, the succession was unclear. Throughout his reign, Edward used the lack of an heir as an incentive to loyalty. It appears that he promised the crown to different people in turn. In 1051, William of Normandy visited Edward. It is possible that the king recognized him as his successor, but no proof exists of this. In 1065, King Edward sent Earl Harold Godwinson to visit William. Norman sources later stated that this was to confirm the naming of William as heir – but again, no evidence survives. Harold Godwinson subsequently reported that Edward had named *him* as his inheritor on his deathbed. The stage was set for the battle of 1066.

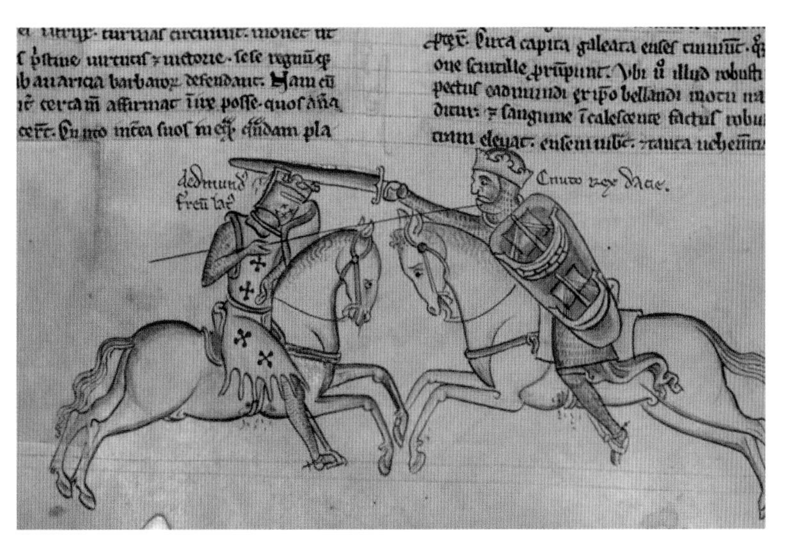

Below: *Edmund Ironside in battle against Cnut at the Battle of Assandun in 1016, from a 14th-century manuscript. Cnut's victory here consolidated Danish rule over England.*

A STRONG KING OR SAINTLY AND WEAK?

The *Anglo-Saxon Chronicle* portrayed Edward as a strong king: 'He in the world here dwelt awhile in royal majesty mighty in council. Four-and-twenty, lordly ruler! of winters numbered, he wealth dispensed; and he a prosperous tide; ruler of heroes, distinguished governed, Welsh and Scots, and Britons also.'[7] Why was he later portrayed as a spiritual man unable to cope with the rigours of kingship? Twentieth-century historian Professor Frank Barlow believed it was because Edward's death led directly to the Norman Conquest. Also, he failed to have children with his beautiful wife; in the late 11th and early 12th century, hagiographers assumed that he had taken a vow of celibacy, but it is more likely that he had no interest in women or that one of the couple was infertile.[8] Edward was canonized in 1161, securing his saintly reputation.

Right: *Edward the Confessor, shown in the first panel of the Bayeux Tapestry. During his reign he began the construction of Westminster Abbey.*

REX:
VBI:

CHAPTER 2

THE NORMANS 1066–1154

The Norman Conquest is commonly viewed as a major turning point in English history. In 1066, William of Normandy subjugated England, establishing a new Anglo-Norman culture and the feudal system. For much of the Norman period, England and Normandy were governed as one empire under a single ruler, but with no rules for the succession to the throne, disputes over the right to the Crown were frequent. England attempted to bring Scotland and Wales under its authority, and tensions between the monarch and the Pope over the control of the Church surfaced. Both issues led to long-running, acrimonious conflicts over the following centuries.

WILLIAM I (1066–87)

William the Conqueror was known as a man you would not want to cross, a harsh ruler who brooked no dissent. 'He was mild to the good men that loved God, and beyond measure severe to the men that gainsaid his will.'[1] When Harold Godwinson seized the crown after the death of Edward the Confessor in January 1066, William of Normandy saw Harold as a usurper. The cousin of Edward, he invaded England; sailing from St Valéry sur Somme in September with a fleet of some 700 ships, he defeated Harold and took control of the country. King William maintained Saxon laws, but introduced the Norman feudal system. Feudalism prevented the monarch from exercising unlimited power, and it laid the foundation for the development of laws regulating the Crown's role.

THE SUBJUGATION OF ENGLAND

The Battle of Hastings was just the start. As William imposed heavy taxes and French nobles came to England to seize land and wealth, Norman rule was extremely unpopular. Over the following six years, William ferociously crushed resistance to his rule; opposition was particularly strong in the north. In 1069, a large Danish army attacked the Yorkshire coast. They were joined by a huge force of English rebels and Edgar Aetheling, provoking an uprising against William in the north of England. The king regained control

Opposite: *A 16th-century portrait of William the Conqueror. For much of his life he was known as 'William the Bastard', a reference to his illegitimate birth to Robert I of Normandy's mistress.*

NORMAN MONARCHS

William I the Conqueror (1066–87)
|
William II (1087–1100)
|
Henry I (1100–35)
|
Stephen (1135–54)

GVLIELMAS · CONQISTER ·

THE BATTLE OF HASTINGS, 14 OCTOBER 1066

'William the earl landed at Hastings, on St Michael's-day: and Harold came from the north, and fought against him before all his army had come up: and there he fell, and his two brothers, Girth and Leofwin; and William subdued this land.'[2]

When William's forces arrived on the south coast on 29 September, King Harold was in the north of England, fighting the Battle of Stamford Bridge against a Viking army. He was forced to march south hastily to confront the Normans. Although his soldiers were exhausted, the battle was closely fought, with thousands killed on both sides. The Normans emerged victorious when Harold fell after being hit in the eye with an arrow.

Above: *The Bayeux Tapestry depicts the death of Harold Godwinson in the Battle of Hastings, 1066.*

and razed York to the ground. His forces laid waste to large parts of Yorkshire and Durham, destroying villages and farmland, and stealing livestock. Famine resulted, and stories emerged of people forced to eat dogs, cats and even human flesh to survive. It is estimated that 100,000 people died.[3]

William now dominated the country. He punished the rebel earls by confiscating their land and giving it to Norman aristocrats, who became nobles of England. But the king ensured that the Norman nobles employed English knights to avoid further division and conflict between the conquerors and the vanquished. In the Norman tradition, William ordered the nobles to build stone castles for protection, and by 1100 there were 500 Norman castles, in the country's major towns and cities, including Exeter, Nottingham, Warwick, London, Lincoln, Cambridge, Huntingdon, Newcastle and at Windsor. He went on to campaign in Scotland in 1071–72, defeating King Malcolm III, and forcing him to sign the Treaty of Abernethy. In return for swearing allegiance to William, Malcolm was given land in Cumbria. Aware of potential external threats, particularly from Denmark, William imposed heavy taxation to pay for bolstered defences. In 1085, he commissioned the 'Great Survey' of landholding in England, primarily to help him to collect tax revenue effectively and also to administer the feudal system.

Above: *The motte and baily section of Windsor Castle, built by William I in the late 11th century, was typical of Norman architecture.*

FEUDALISM AND SOCIAL CHANGE

William introduced the feudal system to maintain centralized authority. Power was based on land ownership, and the king was the ultimate owner of all the land. He granted land to his followers, making sure that no one could concentrate large forces in one area and ensuring that he retained sufficient land to remain more powerful than anyone else. He claimed all the forests too, which covered one-third of the country. In exchange for land, each landowner had to swear allegiance to the king and provide knights when requested for military service. In turn, the landowner gave land to his knights in exchange for their service. Most agricultural labourers became serfs, farming their own land, and also working on the lord's land in return for the right to farm. The system was rapidly introduced in England, but it took centuries to control Wales, Ireland and Scotland and establish feudalism in those countries.

The Norman Conquest brought cultural shifts too. William established his authority over the Church, Saxon bishops were replaced with Normans after they died, and many monks came over from Normandy. The new aristocracy linked to Normandy spoke Norman French, although ordinary people still spoke English. Over time, Anglo-Saxons and Normans began to mix. They intermarried, and the languages

THE NEW FOREST

The New Forest is nearly 1,000 years old: William designated it as his 'new forest' in 1079 having evicted the inhabitants of some 20 small hamlets and isolated farmsteads to create it. At that time, a forest was land for the exclusive use of the monarch for hunting 'beasts of the chase' – mostly deer and wild boar – and included heath as well as woodland. Commoners (those who were neither priests nor nobles) who encroached on Crown land were subject to severe punishment, including the death penalty if they killed a deer.

Left: *The New Forest, covering approximately 150 square miles (380 km²) in Hampshire and Wiltshire, was previously known as 'Ytene', the land of the Jutes.*

began to blend too. New words entered the English lexicon, including many related to administration, such as parliament, government and the crown, and others to do with food production, such as onion, pork and beef.

The king's connections with Normandy led to economic change, as trade between England and Europe expanded. Iron was imported from Sweden and the north of Spain, and fine cloth from Flanders, while wine arrived from Gascony, building stone from northern France, and spices were brought via Europe from south-east Asia. Skilled artisans migrated from Normandy to build castles and churches with the Norman stone. England became visibly different to pre-Conquest times.

Yet, as connections between England and Normandy were deepened, back in France, King Philippe I took advantage of William's absence to attack Normandy. In 1086, William returned to Normandy to fight back, and as his army was sacking the town of Mantes in a retaliatory raid, the king fell ill and died shortly afterwards.

KINGS
LORDS
KNIGHTS
SERFS

Opposite: *Peasants sow seeds in a field outside a medieval town. In the feudal system introduced by the Normans, serfs faced many restrictions.*

THE *DOMESDAY BOOK*

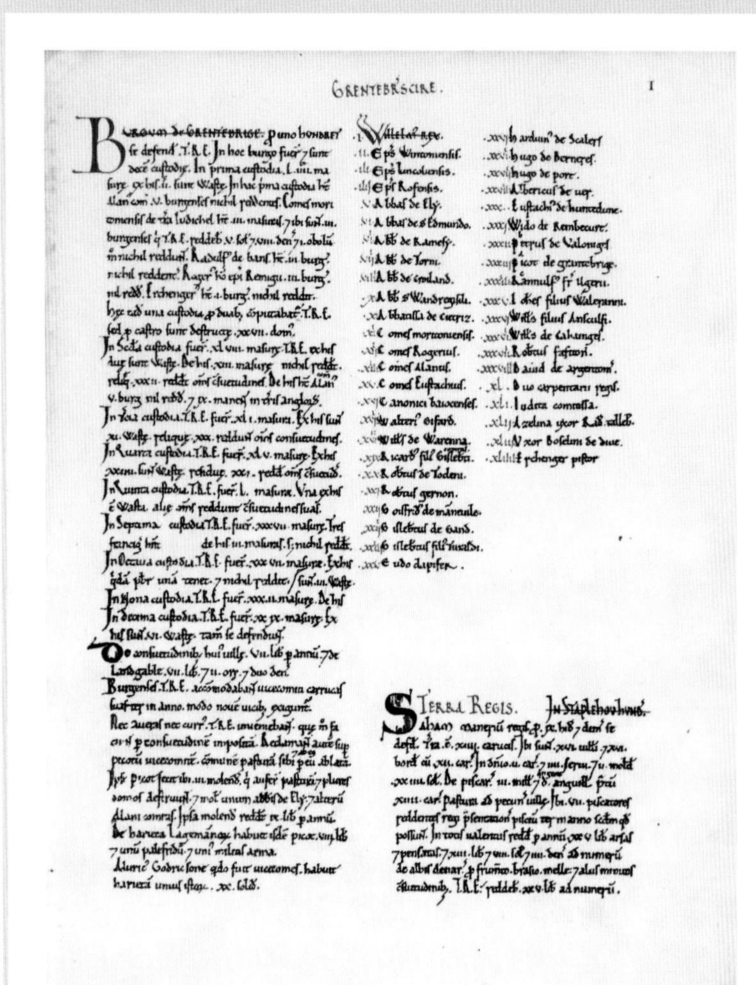
GRENTEBRSCIRE.

I

TERRA REGIS.

The original manuscript, finished in 1086, was a survey of the land and people of England, the first of its kind and the most detailed record produced in medieval Europe. The name, *Domesday Book*, dates to the 12th century; people likened the inspection to the angel of God recording all the facts of their lives for Domesday, the final Day of Judgement. It was certainly detailed. The *Anglo-Saxon Chronicle* stated: 'So very narrowly did he cause the survey to be made that there was not a single rood of land [quarter of an acre], nor… an ox, or a cow, or a pig passed by, and that was not set down in the accounts.'[4]

Left: *The entry from the* Domesday Book *for Cambridgeshire. The* Domesday Book *aimed to provide a detailed listing of all landholdings in the country, to help with matters of taxation and administration.*

WILLIAM II (1087–1100)

A lively character, later nicknamed Rufus for his red hair and ruddy complexion, William II was a notable warrior, possessing the chivalrous qualities of a medieval knight. He has a reputation as brutal tyrant, mainly because the earliest histories of his reign were written by churchmen who disliked him owing to his lack of piety and failure to support the Church. William's reign was dominated by revolts and conflicts with Wales, Scotland and the Church. Despite these struggles, the king was able to maintain law and order and rule effectively.

William I had left Normandy to his eldest son Robert and England to his second son William. It was Norman practice to give land to more than one son but, in this case, it led to serious conflict. Many Norman barons wanted the kingdom to remain united under Robert, while William wanted to control Normandy too. Each brother desired to rule the other's territory to maintain the Anglo-French empire as one. After William fought and overthrew his brother for the control of Normandy in 1089, Norman barons repeatedly led revolts all over England. The king suppressed the uprisings and brutally punished the leaders. To obtain support for his campaign against the Normans, he promised the English nobles fair laws and taxes, and to restore the forests for hunting – although he didn't implement these pledges. The battle for Normandy continued until 1096, when eventually Robert gave up and allowed his brother to rule in return for payment. Normandy remained under English rule for the rest of William's reign.

William was determined to subdue Scotland and Wales. In the 1090s, he defeated the Scottish kings and made them his vassals, and he regained Cumbria from the King of Scots. Thus he became overlord of Scotland. The king extended direct control in Wales. Following conquests in the late 1090s, it was divided into North and South; the South fell under English rule. By 1099, most of Pembroke and Glamorgan was ruled by England, while Powys and Gwynedd retained their independence.[5]

AN IRRELIGIOUS RULER

Unusually for a monarch, William II was cynical about religion and had no esteem for the Church; he seized the revenues of vacant bishoprics and was known as a blasphemer, uttering oaths and obscenities that shocked churchmen. During his reign, male fashions became extravagant and feminine – he never married and was probably gay. Common contemporary opinions of William are summed up in the *Anglo-Saxon Chronicle*: 'In his days therefore, righteousness declined and every evil of every kind towards God and man put up its head.' [6]

TENSIONS WITH THE CHURCH

For most of his reign, the king apparently saw the Church as an asset to be stripped for his own benefit and to help him finance his many wars. William imposed heavy taxes on the monks, earning their resentment, and he sold Church offices or kept them vacant so he could siphon off the income. Stories circulated of churchmen forced to strip out the precious metal from their altars to pay their taxes.

In 1093, when William fell sick and thought he was dying, it seems he decided to change his ways and appoint an Archbishop of Canterbury; the post had been unfilled for four years. He appointed Anselm from Normandy. But the king soon came into conflict with his archbishop, who was critical of William's behaviour towards the Church and maintained his personal allegiance to Pope Urban II in Rome. Anselm's loyalty to the Pope above his king annoyed William – he exiled the archbishop to Rome in 1097 and grabbed the property of the archbishopric. Anselm wisely stayed in Rome to avoid further battles between the Crown and the Church, and was out of the country when the king died suddenly in 1100.

Above: *A 17th-century portrait of William II.*

Right: *An early 17th-century portrait of Henry I.*

HENRY I (1100–35)

Henry seized the throne immediately after his brother's death. He had been well educated, although historians from the 15th to the 19th centuries exaggerated his skills, asserting that he had mastered Ancient Greek and acquired a degree from the University of Cambridge – which did not yet exist. Most contemporaries and modern historians judge Henry as a skilful monarch, who preferred diplomacy to war and was able to reunite the Anglo-Norman state and maintain peace in England. Yet monarchical rule was still based on what historian David Bates describes as 'brute force and personal alliances'.[7]

Since his claim to the throne was precarious, Henry moved quickly to secure support from the nobles. At his accession, he issued a Charter of Liberties: he agreed to end random taxation, the confiscation of Church revenue and the other abuses of power imposed during William II's reign. The Charter later formed the basis of

DID HENRY ASSASSINATE HIS BROTHER?

William II died in a hunting accident in the New Forest, felled by an arrow aimed at a stag by fellow hunter Walter Tirel. William's older brother Robert Curthose was next in line to the throne but was away fighting on the First Crusade. Some historians in the past suggested that Henry, his younger brother, ordered the assassination, but contemporary sources show this is unlikely – the death was reported as an accident. William of Malmesbury wrote an account of Tirel's shot 20 years later: 'Unknowingly and without power to prevent it he sent his fatal arrow through the king's breast.' Although there is no evidence that it was an assassination, Henry rapidly took advantage of the situation.

Right: *An illustration of the death of William II in the New Forest. Walter Tirel fled the scene after the king's death, fuelling the belief that an assassination had taken place.*

Magna Carta (see pages 51–2). The king married Edith (known afterwards as Matilda), sister of Edgar Aetheling – who had briefly been proposed as king after the Battle of Hastings – and daughter of Malcolm III, the King of Scots from 1058–93. Linking himself with a pre-Norman English king strengthened perceptions of Henry's right to the Crown. To deepen his connection with pre-Conquest England, he took charge of the compilation of Anglo-Saxon law and commissioned a history of the English kings, the first extensive account since Bede's eighth-century version. Henry also worked to gain the backing of the Church by recalling the exiled archbishop Anselm in 1100.

Below: *A page from Henry I's Charter of Liberties.*

CONQUEST OF NORMANDY

Robert Curthose returned from the Crusades keen to claim the English crown. He raised an army and landed at Portsmouth in 1101. Though several barons switched allegiance to him, Henry had successfully consolidated his power in England and the revolt came to nothing. He made a settlement with his brother, giving Robert his territories in Normandy and a large annuity; in return, Henry would keep England. However, Robert was a poor ruler and allowed Normandy to slip into chaos. Henry saw his opportunity, and in 1105–6, he subjugated Normandy and dispossessed Robert of his Norman lands. In 1118–19, he fought off an attack in France by an alliance, including the French king Louis VI, to become the most powerful ruler

Right: *A medieval manuscript shows Matilda of Scotland (left) and Henry I (right). Matilda, who was christened as Edith, acted as regent while the king was absent and instituted a major programme of church-building.*

> **CLASH WITH THE CHURCH**
>
> Henry hoped that the Church would shore up his position, yet he argued with Anselm just as his predecessor had done. Anselm believed in the reforms advocated by Pope Paschal II to make the Church independent of royal control. The Pope banned secular lords investing churchmen with land, and churchmen giving homage to secular authorities. Anselm therefore refused to accept bishops that Henry had invested or to offer homage to him. Once more, the archbishop was exiled, from 1103 to 1107. Henry was able to reach a compromise, though. In 1107, he agreed to the Concordat of London, by which he abandoned lay investiture but kept oversight of elections to bishoprics and abbacies. On his part, Anselm agreed to give homage to the king. The tensions between the powers of the English monarchy and the Church abated – for the time being at least.

in Europe. Henry made peace with France in November 1120 and returned to England.

The king was frequently in Normandy, so he developed a system of centralized royal administration to function in his absence. His main motivation was the efficient collection of taxes. A group of advisers acted on the king's behalf, and until her death in 1118, Henry's wife Matilda also helped to maintain royal authority. She attended meetings of the king's council and was well versed in the affairs of state; she frequently chaired the gatherings when Henry was away. To keep an eye on finances, the exchequer was introduced – a royal accounting system – with annual audits called pipe rolls. Henry appointed royal justices to tour the shires to support local administrators and check they were collecting revenue effectively. An unintended by-product of Henry's innovations was a move away from personal control by the sovereign towards a state bureaucracy.

Henry planned ahead for the succession. He married his daughter Matilda to Emperor Henry V of Germany and named his son William as his heir, but William perished in the shipwreck of the *White Ship* in 1120. After Henry V died in 1125, the king summoned his daughter back and named her as his successor. Yet when Henry passed away, his nephew Stephen of Blois ignored Matilda's right to the throne and took it for himself.

KING STEPHEN (1135–54)

Like the previous two kings, King Stephen usurped the throne. The nephew of Henry I, he raced to London on Henry's death to claim the throne, forswearing his oath of 1127 to accept Henry's daughter Matilda as the next monarch. Controversy among historians about his reign has abounded. Contemporary accounts told of violence, disorder and weak kingship, and 19th-century historians described Stephen's failure to inspire loyalty. In contrast, recent historians appreciate that Stephen had complex problems to cope with: the disputed succession, powerful rivals and the challenge of being the first monarch to succeed in both England and France simultaneously.

THE 'ANARCHY'

Matilda was not prepared to renounce her claim to the throne, and in 1138 her half-brother, Robert, Earl of Gloucester, rebelled against Stephen on her behalf. The following year, Matilda invaded England, and civil war broke out. Stephen allowed Empress Matilda and Earl Robert to travel from Arundel to Bristol rather than imprisoning them, hoping that permitting the rebels to gather in one region of the country would make it easier to defeat them. Instead, the pair gathered support in western England. Stephen was captured in 1141, and it appeared he would lose the throne.

Yet Matilda could not gain enough support to be crowned queen; her arrogant behaviour angered her followers. People of the City of London were furious at her proposition to levy taxes on them to restore the depleted royal coffers, and she was ejected from London by a riot. The throne was still disputed however, and Matilda's son Henry, ruler of Normandy, attacked England in 1147 and 1149, both times unsuccessfully. In the early 1150s, Henry became Duke of Normandy, inherited Anjou from his father and married Eleanor of Aquitaine. As lord of a great swathe of French territory, he was now a power to be reckoned with, and his 1153 invasion of England offered the possibility of reuniting England and Normandy. This time, peace terms were finally agreed. Stephen was to remain king for his lifetime and then Henry would succeed. Stephen had been unable to overcome his rivals, and his experiences indicated that without negotiation and compromise, it was impossible for a monarch to rule effectively.

Left: *King Stephen (left) in a manuscript from the late 13th century. Contemporaries viewed him as mild-mannered and weak.*

THE SINKING OF THE *WHITE SHIP*

On the day Henry secured a peace agreement with France, his heir William Aetheling was celebrating his father's victory with his companions aboard the *White Ship* as it left the harbour in Barfleur, Normandy. The crew joined in the wine drinking and merriment, and failed to notice an underwater rock a short distance out of the harbour. The *White Ship* crashed into the rock, killing virtually all aboard; the sole survivor was said to be a butcher from Rouen.

Above: *Detail of the wreck of the* White Ship, *from a 14th-century manuscript.*

Chapter 3

The Struggle for Power in Wales 800–1536

The Welsh kingdoms were founded around AD 400, after the fall of Roman rule. Wales was home to the Brythonic people, who spoke Brythonic, a Celtic language that developed into modern Welsh. On the other side of the Welsh border lived the Anglo-Saxon people. In the late 8th century, Offa, ruler of the Anglian kingdom of Mercia, constructed Offa's Dyke, a huge earthwork structure running along the modern border between Wales and England. Built from sea to sea, it was intended as a boundary between Offa's kingdom and Powys on the Welsh side. It helped to define the territory of Wales.

MAIN WELSH KINGS AND PRINCES (800–1284)

Rhodri Mawr (844–78)
|
Hywel Dda the Good (915–50)
|
Gruffudd ap Llywelyn (1039–63)
|
Gruffudd ap Cynan (1081–1137)
|
Owain Gwynedd (1137–70)
|
Llywelyn ap Iorwerth the Great (1194–1240)
|
Llywelyn ap Gruffudd the Last (1246–82)

Left: *Dinefwr castle was the seat of Hywel Dda. According to tradition, a castle was built on this site by his grandfather Rhodri Mawr, though no parts of this older castle remain.*

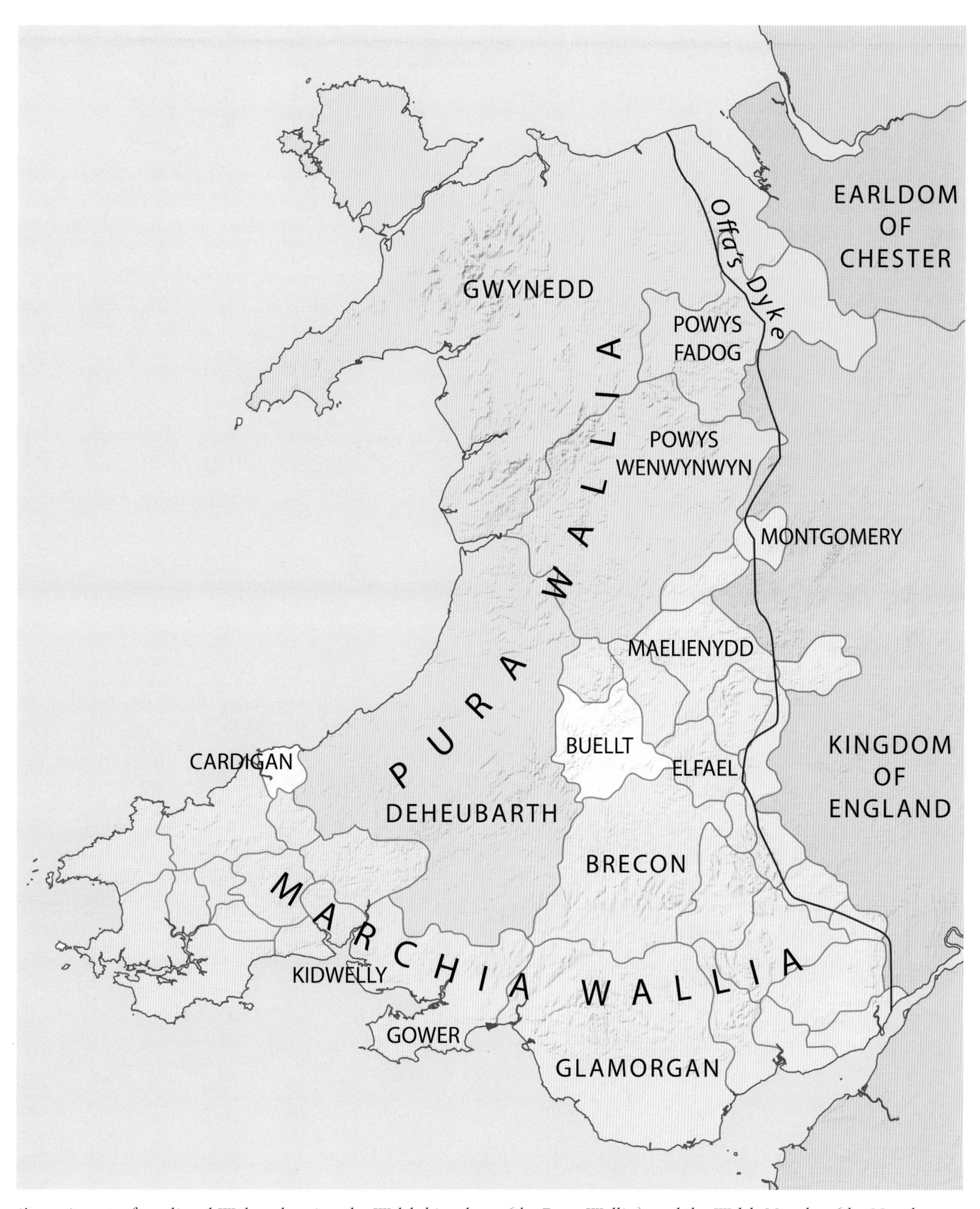

Above: *A map of medieval Wales, showing the Welsh kingdoms (the Pura Wallia) and the Welsh Marches (the Marcha Wallia) established by autonomous Norman lords, as well as Offa's Dyke, which divided Wales from England.*

By the 9th century, the Welsh state had started to emerge, and Wales came under a single ruler. Revered for his bravery in battle, Rhodri Mawr, King of Gwynedd, resisted Viking attacks; in 856 he achieved victory over the Viking leader Orm, slaying him in battle on Angelsea, and brought Powys and Seisyllwg (later Cardigan and Carmarthen) into his kingdom. This union between South and North ended when he was killed fighting the English in 878, but his grandson Hywel Dda revived it in the 10th century. Wales became fully unified in 1057 under Gruffudd ap Llywelyn, who extended control over the whole country. During the following centuries, the rulers of England set their sights on dominating Wales.

Above: *Hywel Dda from one of the 13th-century* Peniarth Manuscripts. *During his reign, he developed a close relationship with King Athelstan of England.*

COEXISTENCE OR CONFLICT

Some Welsh kings opted for cooperation with their powerful neighbours, while others chose the path of resistance. Hywel Dda recognized the English king as overlord. In contrast, Gruffudd ap Llywelyn resolved to unite Wales, invading territories that had been lost to England. Harold, Earl of Wessex, retaliated by invading Wales in 1063, killing the Welsh leader and weakening the opposition.

After the Normans conquered England in 1066, they pushed into Wales too. But Wales was far more decentralized than England and harder to control. In the late 11th century, the Welsh revolted against the Normans, driving them out of Gwynedd, Ceredigion and most of Powys. Wales became divided between regions held by the Welsh and lordships ruled by Normans. The Norman areas became known as the Welsh March – they were independent kingdoms, with their own courts and castles.

RECONCILIATION OF RIVALS

Hywel Dda is known for codifying Welsh law, around 940. His law focused on reconciling rival groups rather than punishing wrongdoers. Crime was perceived as an offence against the family not the state. If someone killed or injured a person, their family had to offer compensation to the individual or their relatives – the amount depended on the social status of the victim. The body of a free man was valued at 3,780 pennies, or 63 cows.[1] The compassionate nature of Hywel Dda's laws earned him the nickname 'the Good'.

MANORIALISM

The Norman incursions changed social relations in the regions they held. In 1000, Wales was a rural society; there were no towns. The Welsh people were either free or unfree: landowners were free, and they allocated land to the unfree, who had to pay for it with food and services. The Normans introduced the manorial system, in which landowning was linked to military service. The land was divided into areas called knights' fees, each one supporting a mounted warrior. The manor was maintained by villeins, unfree labourers who worked the land. Increasingly, villeins had to give money to the lord rather than payment in kind. The Normans also swept aside the principles of Welsh law. Rather than being considered an offence against kin, crime was defined as a transgression against the ruler.

In the 13th century, English kings made a concerted effort to conquer the whole of Wales. Llywelyn ap Gruffudd tried to come to an accommodation with the English monarchs, but when they proved overbearing, he fought back. In 1267, he recognized the overlordship of Henry III. Yet English royal officials intervened in Welsh affairs, leading to growing resentment. In 1282, a rebellion spread across most of Wales, and Llywelyn ap Gruffudd took up leadership of the revolt. Despite fierce resistance, Edward I of England succeeded in his aim to subjugate the kingdom. English law was extended to Wales through the Statute of Rhuddlan in 1284, and Edward made Wales his principality.

Below: *The tomb of Gruffudd ap Llywelyn. He united Wales in 1057.*

THE REVOLT OF OWAIN GLYNDWR

In 1399 Henry IV seized the throne from Richard II (see page 79) but struggled to consolidate his power in Wales. Many Welsh nobles had links with Richard and felt little allegiance to Henry, so resentment of English rule was widespread. Owain Glyndwr saw an opportunity to throw off the English yoke.

In 1400 supporters of Owain Glyndwr proclaimed him Prince of Wales. Using guerrilla hit-and-run tactics, they attacked English settlements in North Wales, and the following year, Glyndwr's allies occupied Conwy Castle. The country descended into civil war as some Welsh people remained loyal to England. Henry IV led campaigns against Glyndwr, but could not defeat his guerrilla forces or cope with the terrible weather conditions. His government passed a punitive Penal Code that prevented the Welsh from gathering, carrying arms or living in fortified towns. Over the next few years, the balance of power shifted towards Glyndwr, who was acknowledged by most of Wales as ruler in 1405. But from 1408 to 1410, the new English king, Henry V, reasserted supremacy over the country, and Glyndwr was forced to flee. The conflict had proved devastating for the economy, and in the end, the Welsh gentry decided it was wise to cooperate with the English rulers.

Above: *Conwy Castle was built by Edward I between 1283 and 1289. In 1401, it was held for several months by Owain Glyndwr's forces.*

Opposite: *A bronze statue of Owain Glyndwr. He was the last native Welshman to hold the title of Prince of Wales.*

MAGIC AND TRICKS

Some English opponents of Owain Glyndwr believed he was able to control the weather to impede their campaign. It was thought that he had his horse shoed back to front so that the tracks would indicate he was travelling in the opposite direction, and that he stuck poles in the ground with hats on, so that the enemy would think he had a huge army. The English were never able to capture Glyndwr. After the rebellion, he simply vanished and no record exists of where he died. Consequently, he gained mythical status, with many believing that he was resting in a cave somewhere, awaiting the call from his country to lead a renewed revolt.

Left and below: *The two sides of the seal of Owain Glyndwr.*

POETRY AND RESISTANCE

Between 1100 and 1300, the Welsh princes patronized Welsh-speaking poets as part of the development of a national culture. One of the finest poems was 'The Elegy of Gruffudd ab Yr Ynad Coch to Llywelyn ap Gruffudd'. The third stanza talks of the 'dark hand' of Saxon rule over Wales after Llywelyn ap Gruffudd was struck down in 1282:

What now for us left
with a full load of weeping?
The dark hand that felled him
haunts his kingdom; his hall now the grave.
A long vista of fear stretches before us.[2]

THE TUDORS – A WELSH DYNASTY

The Wars of the Roses (1455–85) had a significant impact on Wales. At first, the Welsh principality favoured the Lancastrians, while the March was loyal to the Yorkists – especially the Mortimer lordships, because the Yorkists were descended from the Mortimer family. The eventual victor was the Lancastrian Henry Tudor, who took the throne in 1485. Of Welsh and French descent on his father's side, Henry VII controlled most of Wales: the principality and all the lordships of the March. However, he maintained the Council of Wales and the Marches (a form of regional government established in 1472 which mostly dealt with imposing law and order). Henry's Welsh roots helped to ensure that the Welsh gentry became loyal to the Tudor dynasty, and rebellions in Wales did not continue as they did in Ireland.

THE ACT OF UNION, 1536

The following Tudor monarch, Henry VIII, desired sovereignty of the Crown throughout his kingdom, and in 1536 Wales was united with England. The Act of Union divided the March into seven counties, so there was no longer any difference between the principality and the lordships of the March. The laws of England became the laws of Wales, Justices of the Peace were appointed in every county, and English became the language of the courts. Wales had 26 MPs to represent the country in Parliament. A further Act of 1543 established the system of Welsh courts and recognized the Council of Wales at Ludlow, which had administrative and legal powers over Wales and gave Wales one more MP.

Below: *Ludlow Castle in Shropshire. This was the seat of the Council of Wales, the body responsible for the government of Wales from the reign of Henry VIII.*

CHAPTER 4

THE HOUSE OF ANJOU 1154–1272

The House of Anjou began with Henry II, through his mother Matilda, daughter of Henry I and a member of the House of Normandy, and through his father Geoffrey Plantagenet, of the House of Anjou. Under this royal dynasty, the links between England and France were strengthened and English monarchs expanded their territory in France. The Angevin kings believed they ruled by divine right, that their actions were directed by God and that they were above all people and the law. However, the legal relationship between the monarchy and the law altered in the 12th and 13th centuries. At the start of the dynasty, kings could indeed act above the law yet by the end, the law had some control over their power, notably through the introduction of Magna Carta in 1215. A single legal system across the country was established too. Frictions emerged over who should exercise authority over religious practice – the monarchy or the Church; the disputes formed the background to the separation of England from the Catholic Church in the 16th century.

ANJOU MONARCHS

Henry II (1154–89)
|
Richard I (1189–99)
|
John (1199–1216)
|
Henry III (1216–72)

Note: The House of Anjou, or the Angevin dynasty, is also known as the House of Plantagenet. The House of Anjou can refer to the entire succession from 1154 to 1485 or just to the line of four monarchs from Henry II through to Henry III, as listed here.

Above: *An illustration from the 14th-century* Grandes Chroniques de France *shows King Philip Augustus of France (left) sending an envoy to Henry II and Queen Margaret of England.*

Opposite: *The descendants of Henry II of England from the* Genealogical roll of the kings of England, *a manuscript from the early 14th century.*

Henry II (1154–89)

Generally a gentle and approachable man, Henry was restless, unable to keep still and had a ferocious temper; once in a rage he 'fell out of bed screaming, tore up his coverlet, and threshed around the floor, cramming his mouth with the stuffing of his mattress'.[1] Nevertheless, he was a strong, capable ruler who restored order after the civil war of Stephen's kingship and reformed the royal finances and the judicial system – despite spending just 14 of his 35 years on the throne in England. He became embroiled in conflict with his archbishop and the papacy over control of the Church and faced rebellions from his wife and sons, who allied with the King of France to bring about his downfall.

SECURING POWER AND MONEY

On his accession, ensuring the loyalty of his subjects was Henry's main priority. During Stephen's reign, nobles with hereditary titles had taken on sheriffs' jobs; the king now appointed his own men to reclaim jurisdiction over the local areas. Furthermore, he took control of the royal castles and had unauthorized ones destroyed to weaken alternative power bases. (He ordered the destruction of Scarborough Castle, but once he realized it was in a valuable strategic position, he changed his mind and instead took over the fortress and extended it.) It was a gamble that could have led the barons to rise up, but fortunately for Henry, they complied. Mutual suspicion of each other was the key – no one dared to be the first to defy the king in case nobody else followed suit. By 1155, King Henry had secured England. He also focused on conquering French territory. In the first three years of his kingship, he secured control of Normandy, Anjou and Aquitaine and received homage from the King of France, uniting England, Normandy and western France under his rule.

To defend his kingdom, Henry allowed the English barons to pay scutage (shield money) instead of providing army service and used the proceeds to hire soldiers when he needed an army. This worked better than using feudal armies: knights owed military service to their lords but had to serve for only 40 days in a year – often not long enough for an expedition to France. With the barons making payments with coinage rather than in kind, the use of money in general expanded. It was an unintentional by-product of royal policy and led to a significant change in customs.

COMMON LAW

Henry's greatest impact was in the reform of royal justice. Modern historians see him as the founder of English Common Law, the origin of a single legal system. He sent a group of justices around the country to bring royal justice at events called eyres. They held the authority to act in the king's name and make judgements. Before, local men had made judgements according to custom, although within the bounds of certain norms. Sending out royal justices regularly around the country ensured the uniformity of the administration and was a vital part of the development of the modern judicial system.

THE 'TURBULENT PRIEST'

Religious reform was not within Henry's control though. External factors laid the ground for the conflict between Henry II and his chancellor Thomas à Becket. The papal reform movement was pushing for the Church to be above the jurisdiction of secular monarchs. This principle tested Becket's loyalty to his king, particularly after his appointment as Archbishop of Canterbury in 1162. The following year, Henry requested that some fraudulent clerks be handed to the secular authorities for punishment, but Becket contended that they should be subject only to Church law. The king became angry that his chancellor was turning against him; Becket kept changing his mind, accepting Henry's proposals and then rejecting them, causing great irritation. At this time, the king is alleged to have made the infamous comment, 'Will no one rid me of this turbulent priest?' He sent knights to Canterbury to deal with Becket and to persuade him to submit to

THE ROYAL MINT

Henry took firm control of the royal finances through the exchequer, and the coffers filled. He also centralized the currency and improved the quality of the coinage. Since the Norman Conquest, powerful families had controlled the mints in various towns and cities. In 1158, the king dismissed the lot of them and selected just a few manufacturers to produce a new silver penny – classified as the 'Cross-and-Crosslets' in the 20th century. It was a clear assertion of Henry's economic power.

Above: *A 'Cross-and-Crosslets' silver penny from the reign of Henry II.*

Above: *An illustration from a 14th-century copy of* The Book of Hours *shows the killing of Thomas à Becket in Canterbury Cathedral.*

CHURCH vs STATE

The philosopher John of Salisbury was an associate of Becket's during his conflict with the king. As secretary to Archbishop Theobald, he outlined the issue in a letter from the archbishop to Henry II:

> *When the members of the Church are united in loyalty and love, when princes show due reverence to priests, and priests render faithful service to princes, then do kingdoms enjoy that true peace and tranquillity that must always be the goal of our desire. But if they clash, one against the other, in all their might, then the vigour of the secular power will be impaired no less than the ecclesiastical.*[2]

Salisbury subsequently backed Becket's cause and the liberty of the Church against the king, and spent much of the 1160s in exile in France or the papal court for doing so.

the king's will. Legend has it that they entered the cathedral without their swords, confronting the archbishop and ordering him to attend the Winchester parliament and explain his actions. When he refused they collected their swords, and cut him down inside the cathedral. After Becket's murder, a cult developed around him, and the cathedral, already a favourite destination for Christian pilgrims, became even more popular as they flocked to visit his tomb. The following year, the king did penance on the spot where the chancellor met his fate to revive his tarnished reputation.

Despite this ill-fated altercation, Henry II continued to interfere in the Church, appointing his own men to important positions and allowing bishoprics and abbey positions to remain vacant so he could obtain the revenue.

REBELLIOUS FAMILY

Henry proved unable to resolve conflict within his own family. He had several sons, which was desirable to ensure the succession to his lands. Yet having several restless offspring waiting for lengthy periods to gain power proved problematic. Henry decided to divide his lands: his eldest son Henry would receive England and Normandy; Aquitaine would go to Richard; Geoffrey was offered Anjou, and Irish territory was to be John's. But although young Henry was made co-regent with his father in 1170, he had no power. All four siblings were dissatisfied with their lot, and in 1173, Queen Eleanor fled with them to the court of Louis VII in France, where they raised a rebellion. Henry took an army to France and defeated them; he made peace with his sons, but imprisoned his wife Eleanor. Yet further battles between Henry and his sons in France ensued over the following 15 years. In 1189, he was at war in France once more, against his son Richard, who had allied with the French King Philip to attack Normandy. Henry was killed in battle, dying in a confrontation over territory with his immediate family.

RICHARD I (1189–99)

Known for his bravery in battle, Richard was nicknamed 'the Lionheart'. Following a brief visit to England for his coronation, he embarked on the Third Crusade to recover Jerusalem for Christianity in 1190; for him, this religious duty was of paramount importance. Richard believed in sharing the risks he imposed on his soldiers. Once he went on an ill-advised mission to rescue a foraging party, explaining, 'I sent those men there. If they die without me, may I never again be called a king.'[3] In his absence, Richard made Hubert Walter chief officer of the crown and left him to govern England and raise funds for the royal military expeditions.

A KING'S RANSOM

While Richard was on the Third Crusade, his brother John plotted with Philip II of France to divide Richard's kingdom. As Richard was returning from the Holy Land in December 1192, he was hunted down, captured and sold to the Holy Roman Emperor Henry VI, who demanded a huge ransom. John spotted an opportunity: in 1193, he travelled to England, stated that Richard was dead and claimed the throne. But no one believed him; if they harboured even a modicum of suspicion that Richard still lived, it would have proved unwise to join a rebellion against a king on crusade, a treasonable act. Convinced his master still lived, Hubert Walter raised the ransom money, and Richard was set free the following year, escorted back to England by his mother Eleanor of Aquitaine. The king spent the rest of his life fighting to recapture French territory that Philip II had appropriated in his absence. In 1196, he gave up the Angevin claim to Toulouse to focus on fighting in the north of France, and it was there that he died in battle in 1199.

Opposite: *A statue of Richard I stands outside the Houses of Parliament in Westminster.*

ELEANOR OF AQUITAINE

Above: *The tomb of Eleanor of Aquitaine in Fontevraud Abbey in France. While Queen of France, she participated in the Second Crusade.*

In the 12th century, Queen Eleanor was perhaps the most powerful woman in Europe. Between 1154 and 1173 she participated in ruling England despite her frequent pregnancies (she and Henry II had eight children). She was responsible for issuing writs and documents in her own name as well as witnessing royal charters, and was involved in making dynastic marriages for her children. Eleanor was a great patron of poetry, sponsoring poets in the two poetic movements of courtly love and the legends of Brittany; the best-known troubadours attended her court at Poitiers. Following the 1173 revolt, Henry imprisoned her until his death nearly 16 years later, after which the septuagenarian resumed her political role, assisting her son Richard in the administration of the kingdom.

THE CRUSADES

During the late 11th century, armies from Western European countries sent crusades to the Middle East to try to halt the expansion of Islam, which had been spreading rapidly for the previous 400 years. These expeditions aimed to maintain Christian control of the Holy Land, the birthplace of Jesus. The Battle of Hattin in 1187 proved to be a turning point: Muslim leader Salah ad-Din defeated the crusader armies and was then able to wrest Jerusalem from the Christians and retake a great part of the Crusader states, ending their occupation of the Holy Land. This led to the Third Crusade, an attempt to defeat Salah ad-Din. The European armies conquered most of the areas that Salah ad-Din had taken, although they were unable to reconquer Jerusalem.

Above: *The 13th-century* Chronica maiora *illustrates a scene from the crusades, showing the Muslim leader Salah ad-Din capturing the Holy Cross.*

The English people paid the price of Richard's military ventures. To raise the king's ransom, subjects were forced to pay an extortionate 25 per cent tax on the value of rents and moveable goods. After the king's release, his ministers resorted mostly to traditional taxation methods, such as scutages, but also to some creative fundraising. People who believed they had bought their offices in 1189 were informed five years later that the offices had only been leased, and the lease had to be renewed. Yet despite resentment of the costs, there was general acceptance that heavy taxation was necessary to fund the campaigns in France and the Holy Land. And the fact that taxes were collected so efficiently indicates that Richard had selected capable officials who ran an effective administration without his presence.

POGROMS

Above: *Clifford's Tower, the keep of York Castle, where 150 Jews were killed in a pogrom in 1190.*

Although Richard's crusading had a positive effect on the development of government administration, it had a disastrous impact on the 2,500-strong Jewish population. Jewish people had arrived from Normandy after 1066. The Norman kings needed to borrow money for building castles, but since Christians were forbidden to lend money, they relied on Jewish moneylenders, who received the Crown's protection. Yet hostility towards the Jews arose in the 12th century because of theological arguments with Christians. When two Jewish citizens arrived with gifts at Richard's coronation, resentment at their presence led to anti-Semitic riots. Richard had some of the rioters hanged and demanded that the Jews be left in peace, but when he departed on crusade, Jewish people lost their protection. In York, the Jews escaped assault by gathering in Clifford's Tower, but were besieged by a mob. Contemporary historian William of Newburgh described how:

> *... in consequence of the want of a sufficient supply of food, they would, without doubt, have been compelled to surrender, even if no one had attacked them from without, for they had not arms sufficient either for their own protection, or to repel the enemy.*

They decided that:

> *... if we should fall into the hands of the enemy, we should die according to their pleasure, and amidst their mockery. Therefore, let us willingly and devoutly, with our own hands, render up to Him that life which the Creator gave to us.*[4]

They killed themselves rather than surrender and be murdered.

JOHN (1199–1216)

Above: *King John is shown in a hunting scene in the illuminated manuscript* De Rege Johanne. *He had a troubled reign and was briefly excommunicated by Pope Innocent III.*

The youngest of Henry II's restive sons, John had attempted to seize the throne before in a treacherous action against his brother Richard. He failed spectacularly; as Richard wryly commented, 'my brother John is not the man to win lands by force if there is anyone at all to oppose him'.[5] Yet John regained his brother's trust during the last few years of the latter's reign and was named his heir. Once John became king by right, he was determined to secure his dominions, whatever the cost. John has a poor reputation for imposing onerous taxation on the barons, and the dispute over his right to do so led to Magna Carta.

RAISING REVENUE

As soon as King Philip had learnt of Richard's death, he invaded Normandy, and John hurried to France to fight him. King John lost all French land except Aquitaine in the war, surrendering Normandy in 1204. With the loss of most of France, he could raise money only in England. To squeeze more out of his subjects, he invented new arbitrary charges for marriage and wardship and extracted the maximum possible feudal payments; he added new taxes – thirtieths, sevenths and even fourths of tenants' incomes, and made frequent demands for scutage. If the barons refused to pay, the king punished them or seized their property. With these unpopular methods, the king quadrupled his takings at the exchequer from 1204 to 1211. In 1213, the Crown possessed almost half of all the money circulating in the country. The king was stockpiling so much money that it caused deflation, and it became hard for people to pay their debts to the Crown.[6]

Below: *A 19th-century illustration of King John signing the Magna Carta at Runnymede in 1215. Runnymede was neutral ground, halfway between Windsor Castle and the stronghold of the rebel forces at Staines.*

MAGNA CARTA

In 1214, the king demanded a further scutage. This was the last straw, which led to a baronial revolt. The barons' forces captured London and demanded a charter of liberties to end the king's right to arbitrarily raise taxation and to subject him to the rule of law. The charter had a security clause that empowered a council of 25 barons to supervise the king's actions and bring him to account if he did not respect their rights and liberties. It ended the monarch's right to freedom of action. Faced with the threat of civil war, the king submitted to the barons and signed the Magna Carta on 15 June 1215.

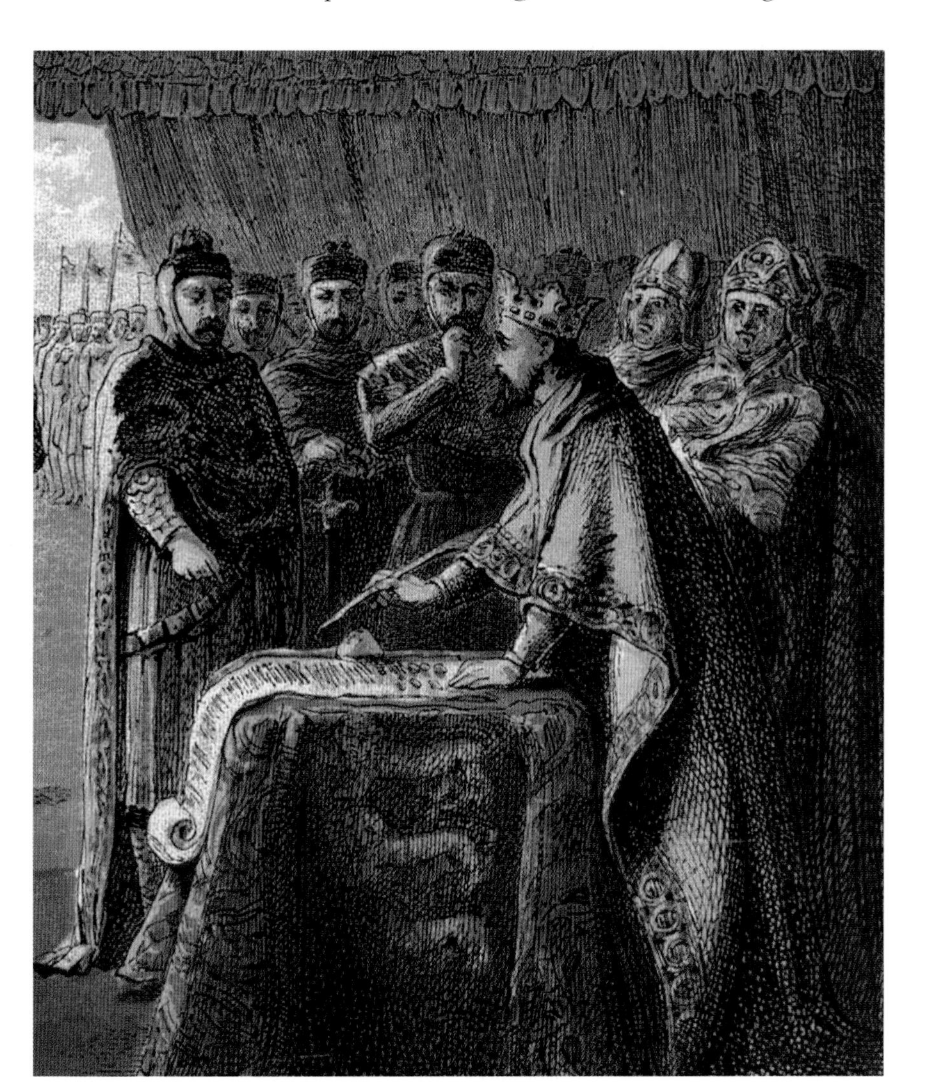

John had no intention of sticking to the charter, however, and he gathered an army to fight the barons, with some success. The rebellious barons offered the crown to the French prince Louis, who arrived in England with a large force. Many formerly loyal barons now deserted the king. John remained determined to fight to retain his kingship, but in autumn 1216, he contracted dysentery and died. Historian S. D. Church suggests that the bad timing of his death helped account for the severe criticism his reign has attracted in the history books. If he had survived and maintained hold of his country, it might perhaps have been a different story.[7]

MAGNA CARTA: CAUSES AND CONSEQUENCES

Was Magna Carta brought about because John was a particularly ineffectual king who levied such extensive taxes that he triggered a rebellion? Or was it inevitable that the powerful barons would have contested demands for taxation from any monarch and sought to limit royal authority? Either way, the absolute power of monarchy was curtailed under John's rule. Although the charter focused on maintaining the privileges of the Norman barons, the subordination of the king to the law can be seen as the origin of constitutional monarchy. It also contained a clause that remains part of the law today: it gave all 'free men' the right to justice and a fair trial. At the time, few people lived in freedom; the majority were unfree serfs, tied to their landlord. Yet as the 20th-century historian Asa Briggs commented, 'the claims for privileges set out in its clauses could in time be translated into a universal language of freedom and justice.'[8]

Below: *One of the few surviving copies of the original Magna Carta of 1215. The charter was revised several times, most notably in 1225, which differed little in content but reaffirmed the limits placed on royal power.*

HENRY III (1216–72)

Henry became king at the age of nine in the midst of civil war. His reign was dominated by a lengthy and unsuccessful war with France, and a continuing power struggle between the monarchy and the barons that temporarily cost him the throne.

When young Henry came to the throne, London and a large area of eastern England were occupied by rebel barons led by Prince Louis of France. In 1217, English forces defeated Louis's army; many rebels returned to the king's side, and Louis withdrew. Henry regained some territory in France in 1225 through war, and then turned to diplomacy. He married Eleanor of Provence in 1236; she had uncles and cousins throughout Europe, which helped Henry form diplomatic links across the continent.

Above: *The coronation of Henry III from a 13th-century manuscript. He became king when he was only nine years old.*

In 1225, Magna Carta was reissued, and for 30 years Henry ruled within its restrictions. He could not levy tax without the consent of a Great Council, a gathering of barons and Church elites. From 1237, the Great Councils were known as parliaments – magnates and prelates were summoned, and from 1265 knights were added to their number. This was the origin of the English Parliament, a permanent restraint on the monarch's power. However, the king put the agreement between the Crown and the barons at risk in 1254, when he agreed to financial obligations he could not possibly meet. He offered the Pope funding for his war in Sicily if the Pope agreed to give the crown of Sicily to Henry's son Edmund. But the king did not come up with the money, and in 1258, the Pope threatened to excommunicate him on failure of payment.

PETITION OF THE BARONS

Henry appealed to the barons, but they would only grant him money if he accepted wide-reaching reforms limiting his power. Their leader, Simon de Montfort, Earl of Leicester, drew up the Petition of the Barons. It included the Provisions of Oxford, which proposed a constitutional monarchy. Reforms would be drawn up by 24 men, 12 chosen by the king and 12 by the barons. Representatives of the 24 would choose 15 men to form the King's Council, which would advise the king and oversee administration. The king could appoint his officers for a year, and they were to answer to the king and the Council. Henry had no choice but to agree with the reforms. The Petition represented a significant restriction of the power of the monarchy, but the new system worked – for a couple of years.

THE FORMIDABLE ELEANOR OF PROVENCE

Following Henry's defeat at the Battle of Lewes in 1264, Queen Eleanor used her network of influential contacts in the papacy and the French court and drew support from Ireland, the Welsh March and English exiles to campaign against Simon de Montfort. She raised a land force to support her husband but needed ships, so she wrote to Alphonse, son of the king of France, to seize British ships to use to transport her army to England:

> *We do not doubt that the iniquity and treason of certain barons of England who strive to disinherit our lord the king of England and his children by open war has reached your hearing and knowledge... Therefore we confidently and assiduously ask your nobility... that you have all the ships of the English that are found in your land and jurisdiction during the said war stopped and detained.*[9]

Alphonse refused her request but she continued indefatigably to seek French aid.

Right: *A 19th-century engraving of Eleanor of Provence.*

Opposite: *A stained-glass window depicting Simon de Montfort in Chartres Cathedral in France. He turned against the king during the 'Mad Parliament' of Oxford in 1258 before eventually raising a rebellion in 1263.*

HALT IN THE MONARCHY

In 1261, Henry repudiated the reforms, the barons rebelled, and in 1264, the king and his son Edward were captured at the Battle of Lewes; Edward was imprisoned. De Montfort became the *de facto* ruler of the country for a year with a council of nine men. His council called together a parliament with two burgesses from selected towns and two knights from each shire. Historian Nicholas Vincent describes it as 'a momentous turning point in English history because De Montfort summoned not just representatives of the counties but also the boroughs.'[10] It indicated the growing importance of the emerging middle class in the communities they represented and their growing power in the land.

However, the kingless experiment did not last. In 1265 Edward escaped, gathered an army, and defeated and killed De Montfort. Henry returned to the throne. Now weak and ill, he allowed Edward to take the reins of government, and he took firm control of the country. Those who had supported De Montford reintegrated into society. Yet the weakness of the royal finances and the financial impact of Edward's decision to go on Crusade in 1268 forced Henry to go cap in hand to Parliament, creating continued tensions between the nascent institution and the monarch.

CHAPTER 5

SCOTLAND: FROM THE VIKING INVASIONS TO INDEPENDENCE 800–1424

Scotland has an impressive tradition of fighting off invaders. From the 1st to the 4th centuries AD, the Romans hoped to conquer the country but proved unable to do so. Over the following few centuries, the Picts, Scots, Britons and Angles gradually merged to create the Scottish kingdom. However, the medieval Scottish kings fought off Viking incursions only to enter into centuries of power struggles with their southern neighbours. After the Norman Conquest, feudalism was introduced, but England's efforts to rule Scotland were continually thwarted, and the country finally gained independence in 1328.

Opposite: *The mighty fortress at Dunnottar in Aberdeenshire, where Constantine repelled a two-month onslaught led by the English king Athelstan in 934.*

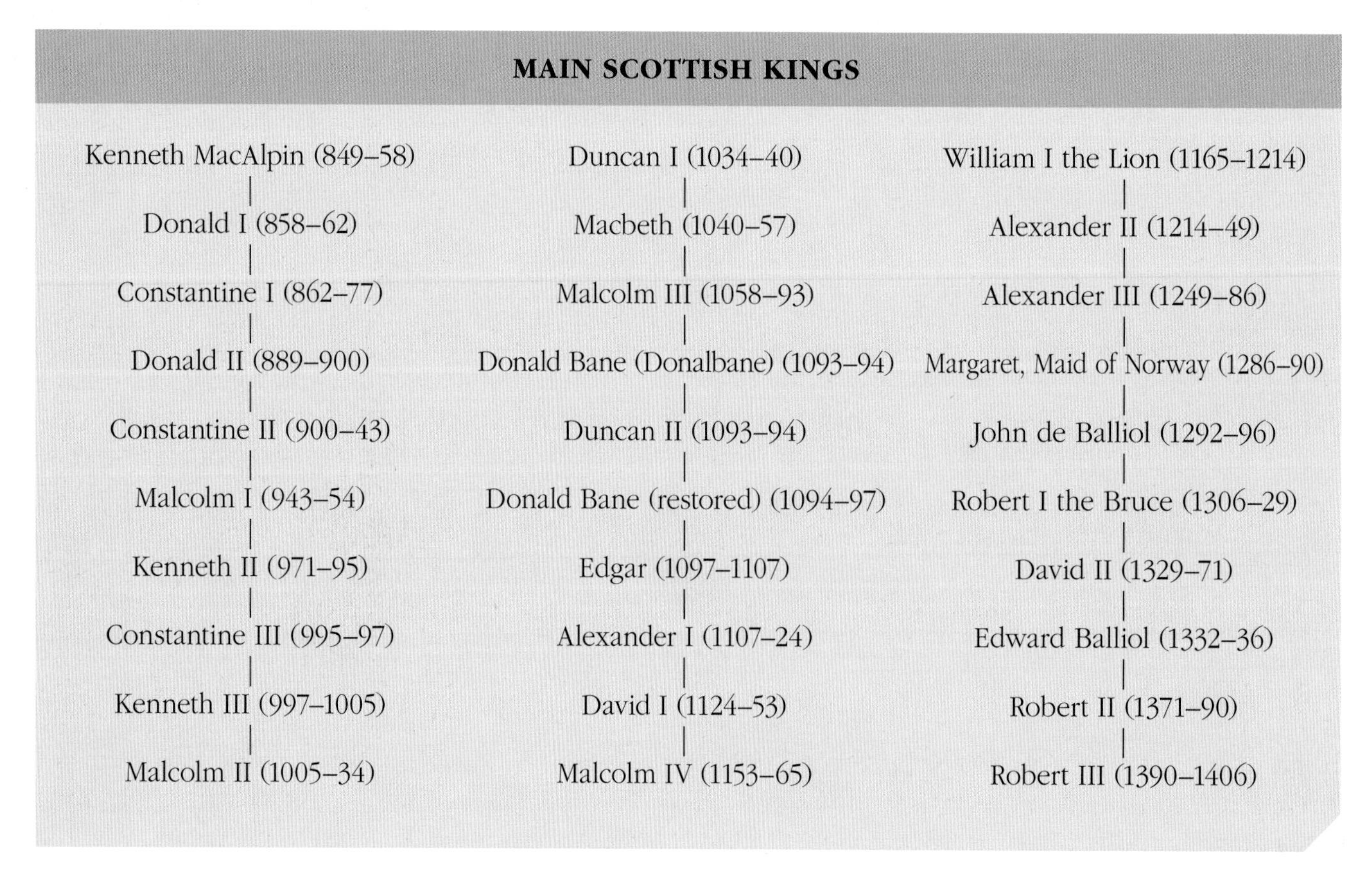

MAIN SCOTTISH KINGS

Kenneth MacAlpin (849–58)	Duncan I (1034–40)	William I the Lion (1165–1214)
Donald I (858–62)	Macbeth (1040–57)	Alexander II (1214–49)
Constantine I (862–77)	Malcolm III (1058–93)	Alexander III (1249–86)
Donald II (889–900)	Donald Bane (Donalbane) (1093–94)	Margaret, Maid of Norway (1286–90)
Constantine II (900–43)	Duncan II (1093–94)	John de Balliol (1292–96)
Malcolm I (943–54)	Donald Bane (restored) (1094–97)	Robert I the Bruce (1306–29)
Kenneth II (971–95)	Edgar (1097–1107)	David II (1329–71)
Constantine III (995–97)	Alexander I (1107–24)	Edward Balliol (1332–36)
Kenneth III (997–1005)	David I (1124–53)	Robert II (1371–90)
Malcolm II (1005–34)	Malcolm IV (1153–65)	Robert III (1390–1406)

ALBA

From the late 8th century, Viking raiders attacked Scotland, seeking plunder to sell and prisoners to enslave. The threat to the kingdom helped to forge unity to defend it. A Scot, Kenneth MacAlpin, established a new dynasty and the supremacy of the Scots' culture and language over the kingdom. The Viking assaults continued; after decades of war, Constantine II defeated the invaders and formed an alliance by marrying his daughters to Viking leaders during the early years of the 9th century. A strong ruler, he brought in a system of mormaers (earls) to defend the kingdom. Constantine called his kingdom Alba – Britain, in Gaelic – and he extended his influence over Scotland through war. He brought much of modern-day Scotland under his control, either directly or as overlord.

BRUNANBURH – THE FIRST 'GREAT WAR'

The *Anglo-Saxon Chronicle* boasted of Constantine's rout at Brunanburh:

'The hoary man of war had no cause to exult
in the clash of blades; he was shorn of his kinsmen,
deprived of friends, on the meeting place of peoples,
cut off in strife, and left his son
on the place of slaughter, mangled by wounds,
young in battle. The grey-haired warrior,
old crafty one, had no cause to boast.'[1]

Then battle with England commenced. In 934, King Aethelstan attacked Constantine at Dunnottar, near Stonehaven, but could not beat him. In return, King Constantine invaded England in 937. Aethelstan retaliated. In a major bloody battle at Brunanburh, his forces met fierce resistance, and both sides experienced heavy losses. Aethelstan vanquished the Scots, but he was weakened and unable to conquer Scotland. As historian Neil Oliver noted, the battle determined that Scotland would remain independent of England for the time being, and the northern land was subsequently ruled by a series of Scottish kings.

Above: *The ruins of Lindisfarne Priory. The Vikings raided the monastery here in 793 before they turned their attention further north.*

FEUDALISM

Scotland could not remain immune from power struggles in England, and the tentacles of the Norman Conquest of 1066 spread northwards; Malcolm III recognized the overlordship of William the Conqueror in 1072. Unwilling to abide by his feudal duties, Malcolm led several attacks on Northumbria, but his incursions failed. During his reign, the foundations of Norman-style feudalism were laid in Scotland. With the encouragement of his queen, Margaret, Malcolm III established abbeys and monasteries, which had an economic as well as a religious function; they farmed the land allotted to them, using peasant labour, and accumulated great wealth. The Church enriched itself further by imposing taxes for religious buildings and upkeep, and for running the institution.

Below: *Malcolm III of Scotland who, together with his queen, Margaret, played a crucial part in the development of medieval Scoland.*

Following the Conquest, Norman nobles moved northwards, took over estates in Scotland and ran them on feudal lines. The peak of the influx occurred under David I (1124–53), who gave land in return for knight service. The incomers created settlements, named after themselves; Duddingston, now in Edinburgh, was named after Dodin. Norman names were introduced too; some historians believe that the surname 'Bruce' was of Norman extraction, originated from the French town of Brix. Under David's successors, the feudal system extended from the royal heartlands to other areas: Strathclyde, Angus, Perth, then Aberdeen and Moray. The older Celtic nobility were displaced.

Well established by the 11th century, the clan networks remained in Scotland alongside feudalism. 'Clann' means 'large family group', and indeed, the clans were originally extended families linked to specific territories.

As the system developed, unrelated families could become associated with a clan for protection. The clan helped people to survive in harsh conditions and times of war, and each one developed its own customs – including the kilts and bagpipes still associated with Scottish tradition today.

Above: *The Benedictine Abbey at Dunfermline was founded by David I in 1128.*

SAINT MARGARET

Known for her great piety, Queen Margaret offered compassion to orphans and the poor, and practised self-denial, including regular fasting. She was determined to bring the Church of Scotland's practices into line with Western Catholicism, encouraging people to take Communion and not to work on Sundays. A popular cult of St Margaret developed after her death, with miracles attributed to her. She was eulogized in the early 12th century, described by Orderic Vitalis as 'eminent for her high birth, but even more renowned for her virtue and holy life'.[2] Eventually, in 1249–50, she was officially canonized.

A stained glass window of Queen Margaret in Edinburgh Castle.

Above: *A fanciful painting of Alexander III by Benjamin West (1738–1820).*

WARS OF INDEPENDENCE

After a relatively peaceful era in Anglo-Scottish relations, a succession crisis revived the conflict. Following Alexander III's death in 1286, guardians ruled Scotland on behalf of his heir, Margaret, Maid of Norway. When she died in 1290, two guardians claimed the throne: John Balliol and Robert Bruce (grandfather of the later and more famous Robert Bruce). They asked Edward I of England to mediate, and his first response was to ask the Scots to accept him as overlord. Balliol and Bruce refused, arguing that his claim was not legitimate.

Backtracking, Edward agreed to judge who should become king of Scotland. He found a host of other claimants, who all vied for his favour. Edward played off the contenders against each other, and eventually judged Balliol to have the best claim in 1292. Although Balliol was installed as king, Edward interfered in Scotland, demanding taxation and Scottish conscripts to join his army in France. In 1295–6, the Scots signed the Auld Alliance with France to shore up their power.

CRUSHED BY EDWARD

The alliance acted like a red rag to a bull: Edward went on the rampage, attacking the important border town of Berwick in 1296. His army stormed the wooden walls and sacked the city, decimating the population. The few survivors were forced to accept English rule. He crushed and humiliated Balliol, stripping him of his crown and insignia and stealing Scottish symbols of identity, including the Stone of Destiny on which kings were crowned. All nobles and senior clergymen had to acknowledge Edward as liege lord. In the face of such a brutal assault, a section of the nobility opted to acknowledge English rule.

Above: *A 14th-century manuscript shows John Balliol kneeling before Edward I.*

UPRISING AND DEFEAT

Yet not all Scots accepted their defeat. A year later, William Wallace and Andrew Murray led an uprising against English rule, in the name of John Balliol. The rebellion also represented a threat to the Scottish nobility who had acquiesced to English dominance. At the 1297 Battle of Stirling Bridge, a small band of spear throwers defeated heavily armed infantry and then cavalry as they tried to cross a narrow wooden bridge. It was the first Scottish victory against the English for hundreds of years, and was a shattering blow to the English army. The following year Wallace was proclaimed Guardian of Scotland. But his triumph was short-lived: in 1298 Edward invaded Scotland and overthrew him. To ensure English domination, Edward attacked Scotland every year for the following six years, wreaking devastation in the southern region. Scottish appeals to France and the Pope fell on deaf ears; both wanted English participation in the Crusades and would not oppose Edward. In 1304, the Scottish nobility submitted to Edward, and those who accepted his rule were rewarded with public office.

WILLIAM WALLACE

The son of a Scottish knight and a minor noble himself, William Wallace of Elderslie was born into a country at war with itself and with the English. Outraged at the Scottish nobles' capitulation to Edward, and opposed to England's punitive taxes and forced conscription, Wallace refused to submit. In May 1297, he assassinated the English High Sheriff of Lanark. His desire for freedom and liberation from Edward's cruelty united the Scottish clans and gained the loyalty of the people. His plea for liberation still has a universal appeal:

This is the truth I tell you:
of all things freedom's most fine.
Never submit to live, my son,
in the bonds of slavery entwined.[3]

In 1304, when Edward demanded loyalty, Wallace refused to compromise and went on the run. He was declared an outlaw and on 3 August 1305, he was captured at Robroyston, near Glasgow. He was then brought to London and tried for treason. The rebel leader was hung, drawn and quartered, then beheaded in the most brutal form of execution. Today, he is remembered as a significant fighter for Scottish independence who died as a martyr to the cause.

Right: *A portrait of William Wallace. Wallace led the victorious Scottish forces at the Battle of Stirling Bridge.*

Left: *A Victorian engraving of the Battle of Stirling Bridge.*

THE MASSACRE OF BERWICK

Scottish historian Walter Bower recounted the massacre in his 1440s *Scotichronicon*:

'When the town had been taken in this way and its citizens had submitted, Edward spared no one, whatever the age or sex, and for two days streams of blood flowed from the bodies of the slain, for in his tyrannous rage he ordered 7,500 souls of both sexes to be massacred... So that mills could be turned round by the flow of their blood.'[4]

STONE OF DESTINY

The origins of the Stone of Destiny are opaque, but this 152-kg (335-lb) block of plain sandstone, decorated with a simple Latin cross, came to be linked to the coronation of Scottish kings. Kenneth MacAlpin brought it to the village of Scone in Perthshire, where it was incorporated into the coronation chair. The stone was later stolen by Edward I to symbolize his dominance of Scotland (see page 62). Since then it has been used in coronation ceremonies for the monarchs of England and Great Britain. On Christmas Day 1950, four Scottish students removed the stone from Westminster Abbey in London. Four months later it was brought back to the Abbey. The British government did not return the stone until 1996. Today, it is on display in Edinburgh Castle, as a potent symbol of the movement for Scottish independence.

Right: *The Stone of Scone, held within the coronation chair at Westminster Abbey, from a 1937 photograph.*

SCOTTISH INDEPENDENCE

The killing of their leaders did not deter the Scots' fight for independence. From 1306, Robert the Bruce led a guerrilla campaign against the enemies of independent rule. After the death of Edward I in 1307, Bruce won back most of the country within six years. At the Battle of Bannockburn in 1314, he defeated an invasion by Edward II designed to relieve Stirling Castle, the last stronghold loyal to England. In the two-day battle, Edward's huge army sustained heavy losses, including thousands of footmen, while Scotland claimed casualties in the hundreds. Bruce now ruled Scotland, although neither England nor the Pope recognized its independence.

Robert Bruce needed this recognition, so the struggle continued. His forces frequently raided northern England, causing widespread destruction, and he invaded Ireland in 1317 to fight the English there as well (although he was forced to retreat the following year). In 1327, Edward II was deposed in favour of his 15-year-old son. Edward III continued to resist the Scottish incursions and was roundly defeated and almost captured in the Stanhope Park campaign in County Durham. Bowing to pressure, England recognized Scotland as an independent kingdom. Yet Scottish liberation was not guaranteed. Over the following 200 years, English armies would continue to invade, not to occupy but to pressurize Scotland to adhere to the monarch's policies.

THE HOUSE OF BRUCE AND THE FIRST STEWARTS

The only surviving son of Robert the Bruce, David II ruled for nearly 40 years, though he spent 18 of those either in exile or in prison. Shortly after he was crowned at Scone Abbey in 1331, a rival claimant to the throne, Edward Balliol, son of John Balliol, invaded Scotland with the aid of an English army –

ROBERT THE BRUCE

In 1306, according to a story of dubious provenance first recounted by Sir Walter Scott in the 19th century, Robert was at a low point, feeling he would never defeat the English. One day, he sat watching a spider repeatedly attempt to attach its web to a beam. Although it seemed like the poor creature would never succeed, eventually its home was complete; the spider's tenacity inspired Bruce to continue fighting for the Scottish kingdom. It may be apocryphal, but nevertheless the tale reflects the determination of the Scottish leader.

Left: *A statue of Robert the Bruce outside Stirling Castle. He ruled Scotland from 1306 until his death in 1329.*

he offered England territory in Scotland in return.

At the Battle of Dupplin Moor in 1332, Balliol achieved a decisive victory. The regent Donald, the Earl of Mar, was killed in battle and Edward was crowned King of Scotland. However, he failed to obtain legitimacy for his rule. In 1336 he was deposed by Sir Andrew Murray and David was reinstated as king in 1341.

In 1346 he joined the French king Philip VI in his war against England. The Scottish forces were defeated, David was captured and spent the next 11 years in captivity. He was restored to the throne in 1357. When he died in 1371, he left no direct heir. Robert II claimed legitimacy as the grandson of Robert the Bruce, but had to fight off armed opposition to take the throne. Although historians in the past regarded him as a weak ruler, recent evaluation indicates that in his reign, Scotland was politically stable with a strong economy, owing to the growth of wool exports.[5]

Robert II's eldest son, John, succeeded him in 1390. He was encouraged to change his name owing to unhappy memories of John Balliol's short reign of 1292–6, and became Robert III. Like his father before him, he was traditionally perceived as a poor leader, but given that he was elderly and ruled at a time of severe economic downturn, the difficulties of his reign cannot be seen as his responsibility alone. In 1406 his son James was captured by the English. Shortly, afterwards, Robert III died; already ill, his heart was broken.

The 12-year-old David thus became King of Scotland, yet he remained a captive of the English king, Henry IV. In his absence, Robert, Duke of Albany, ruled as Regent and Governor of Scotland between 1406 and 1420. He was replaced between 1420 and 1424 by his son Murdoch Stewart, who was unable to rule effectively. The English king finally released James from captivity and he was crowned King of Scotland at Scone in 1424.

CHAPTER 6

THE PLANTAGENETS 1272–1399

In their ambition to unite the British Isles, the Plantagenet monarchs conquered Wales, claimed Ireland and attempted to subjugate Scotland. They also devoted their energies to regaining lost land in France. With little territory in France under English rule, the Plantagenets were forced to rely on English resources for taxation. The institution of Parliament began to develop as an instrument for negotiating with the monarch over the levying of taxes.

EDWARD I (1272–1307)

PLANTAGENET MONARCHS

Edward I (1272–1307)
|
Edward II (1307–27)
|
Edward III (1327–77)
|
Richard II (1377–99)

Note: The name 'Plantagenet' comes from the Angevin symbol, the planta genista – sprig of broom. But the royal family did not use the term before the 15th century.

Nicknamed Edward Longshanks because he was exceptionally tall, Edward I was a successful soldier and ruler from an English viewpoint: he defeated Wales, fought to subdue Scotland and maintained possession of Aquitaine in southern France. In Wales and Scotland his reputation is distinctly less favourable. Under Edward, the institution of Parliament developed, and he established the right of the monarch to raise money to fight wars.

SUBJUGATING WALES AND SCOTLAND

Edward's lasting legacy was the incorporation of Wales into his kingdom (see page 37). In 1284, the Statute of Wales brought Wales into the English legal system and the shire system was introduced; the king built a ring of castles for defence of his newly acquired realm. Edward's experiences in Wales encouraged him to conquer Scotland too, but this would prove a tougher fight. He believed that brute force would do the job but he underestimated the strength of the resistance.

In 1296, Edward defeated his northern neighbour, but his victory sparked a widespread revolt led by William Wallace. He overpowered Wallace at the Battle of Falkirk in 1298 and moved his administration to York to be closer to the scene of action. The king subsequently led annual campaigns to subdue Scotland and succeeded in capturing and executing Wallace in 1305. Edward had finally subordinated Scotland to his rule, although he left much of Scottish law and administration intact and was unable to build defensive strongholds as in Wales because funds were not available for another costly building programme. But the Scots were not so easily crushed. The spirit of rebellion lived on, and from 1305, a new leader, Robert Bruce, intended to retake the Scottish throne. Edward's settlement was left in tatters, and the struggle continued (see pages 64–5).

Opposite: *Edward I was determined to conquer Scotland.*

MAGNA CHARTA
Meeting of Edward & Bruce
Battle of Dunbar
Carnarvon Castle
Queen's Cross
Edward I at Acre

AN 'IRON RING' OF CASTLES

As a display of his dominance, Edward carried out an ambitious castle-building programme, constructing a ring of fortresses in Flint, Rhuddlan, Builth, Aberystwyth, Conwy and other strategic locations. He employed Savoyard master mason James of St George to oversee the work of expert craftworkers from Savoy and English labourers. Unlike earlier square castles, Edward's Welsh fortresses had inner and outer curtain walls and circular towers, adding to their resilience. The costs were enormous, as Master James explained to the king's exchequer when he was building Beaumaris Castle in the 1290s:

Above: *Work on Beaumaris Castle began only in 1295, despite earlier plans, due to an uprising led by Madog ap Llywelyn.*

In case you should wonder where so much money could go in a week, we would have you know that we have needed – 400 masons, both cutters and layers, together with 2000 less skilled workmen, 100 carts, 60 wagons and 30 boats bringing stone and sea coal; 200 quarrymen; 30 smiths; and carpenters for putting in the joists and floor boards and other necessary jobs.[1]

'HAMMER OF THE SCOTS'

Edward died in 1307 while campaigning in Scotland, and he took his obsession with conquering Scotland to the grave; he commanded that he should not have a proper burial until the Scots were vanquished. To this day, his remains are in a plain tomb in Westminster Abbey. The epithet 'Here is Edward I, Hammer of the Scots' was added in the 16th century and the inaccurate nickname stuck – Edward was never able to hammer Scotland into submission.

MONEY FOR WAR

Battle lines were drawn in France too. In 1294, Philip IV of France occupied English-held Aquitaine in southern France. After four bitter years of war, a truce was reached, stipulating that England would maintain control of Aquitaine, and the English Crown would pay homage to the French king, which included a promise not to bear arms against him.

Back home, Edward I accepted the nascent Parliament developed by Simon de Montfort under Henry III and continued to summon the representatives of the towns and lesser knights to Parliament to discuss taxation. He saw Parliament as a 'royal convenience' – an instrument for collecting taxes.[2] It became an important link between economics and politics because the king needed its agreement to finance his military campaigns. Until the 15th century, Parliament gathered wherever the king happened to be at the time. He was frequently in London, and it met at the Palace of Westminster; when he was travelling around the country, Parliament convened in cities such as Winchester, Nottingham and York. From the 15th century onwards, parliaments were generally held at Westminster.

Left: *A page from* Les Très Riches Heures du Duc de Berry *(1412–16) shows sheep shearing. The wool trade was an important part of the medieval economy, on which Edward imposed new taxes.*

Above: *A 14th-century illustration shows Edward I presiding over parliament.*

With wars on so many fronts, Edward frequently summoned Parliament – twice a year up to 1286 – and taxation was extended to raise more money. In Norman times, special taxes had been imposed purely on land, but now that towns were growing, they were levied on property too. Edward was the first monarch to enforce taxes on trade and customs duties; for example, he introduced a new duty on wool and wine sales in 1275. He also seized revenue from the Church to restore his depleted coffers: he stopped paying tribute to the Pope, taxed the clergy without the Pope's permission and grabbed a share of the levies that the Pope charged the clergy.

BATTLING THE BARONS

By 1297, Edward's administration was in major financial crisis. The king had huge commitments and debts owing to his wars in France, Scotland and Wales, but Parliament grew increasingly unwilling to pay. The barons challenged the right of the Crown to use a state of emergency to bypass the normal rules for negotiating over tax and military service. That year, Edward was forced to agree to a Confirmation of the Charters, an affirmation of Magna Carta (see pages 51–2), limiting his right to tax his subjects. He was furious about this restriction of his powers and ignored the charter, creating resentment that would surface again later.

Edward II (1307–27)

The son of Edward I, Edward II has been perceived as a poor ruler who gathered his favourites around him and alienated the barons. A compromise between the demands of the monarch to retain his power and the baronage in Parliament to restrict him proved impossible. The barons rebelled, embroiling England in a civil war, and Edward was eventually deposed.

Conflict arose between the king and the barons after Edward gave the earldom of Cornwall to his great friend Piers Gaveston. The son of a Gascon lord, Gaveston had come to England to seek patronage and his fortune. The political elite resented his meteoric rise to prominence and also wished to limit Edward's power over finances and appointments, especially since he had accrued enormous debts. In 1311, the barons issued the New Ordinances, demanding the banishing of Gaveston and restrictions on the king's control over finances

PETITIONS TO PARLIAMENT

The development of Parliament had an unintended political dimension. When representatives of the shires and towns came to Parliament for discussions about taxation, they often brought petitions from their constituents, and Parliament began to be seen as a forum where the barons could request the king to settle wrongs and offer patronage. The discussion of constituents' concerns in Parliament indicated its potential as an institution for reform.

Left: *The wedding of Edward II and Isabella, from a 15th-century manuscript.*

and appointments. Edward agreed to the terms and exiled his friend. But he immediately began a campaign to annul the Ordinances, and within months he permitted Gaveston to return and restored all lands to him; in revenge, the barons had the lord executed in 1312.

Following Edward's defeat at the hands of Robert the Bruce at Bannockburn in 1314 (see page 64), his rule was weakened, and he was further threatened when a group of barons led by Thomas of Lancaster took control of much of the country in 1315. Lancaster proved to be a poor ruler, though, and by 1318 Edward II had found new favourites to support him, a father and son, both called Hugh Despenser. After several years of civil war, the king crushed his opponents in 1322, executed Lancaster and revoked the Ordinances. Yet his rule remained

PIERS GAVESTON

An unknown writer in Edward's reign described the prince's feelings for Gaveston when he met him around 1300:

> *... upon looking on him the son of the king immediately felt such love for him that he entered into a covenant of constancy, and bound himself with him before all other mortals with a bond of indissoluble love, firmly drawn up and fastened with a knot.*[3]

The relationship between the pair became extremely close although no evidence exists that it was sexual. What is certain is that Gaveston exerted a powerful influence over the king.

THE HUNDRED YEARS' WAR BEGINS

Above: *The Battle of Crécy, shown in Jean Froissart's* Chronicles. *This battle showed the effectiveness of longbows, which would be crucial to English victories at Poitiers (1356) and Agincourt (1415).*

Edward believed he had the right to the French crown through his mother Isabella. Her brother had died without a direct heir and the throne had passed to his cousin. Convinced he was more closely related to the deceased king, he began from 1337 to fight for his claim. He defeated the French at the Battle of Crécy in 1346 and took Calais in 1347, before signing a truce. The next three decades saw Edward gradually lose his gains. In 1359, he gave up his claim to the French throne in return for Aquitaine, but ten years later, the French King Charles V rejected that peace treaty, and France gradually reclaimed Aquitaine. In 1375 a new truce was declared; Edward retained only Calais, Bordeaux, Bayonne and Brest.

Opposite: *The execution of the Earl of Lancaster as portrayed in the* Lutrell Psalter.

insecure. Edward's wife Isabella became the lover of one of his exiled enemies, Roger Mortimer, who was living in Paris. In 1326, Mortimer and Isabella led an invasion of England and executed the Despensers. In 1327, they deposed King Edward, sent him to prison, where he died, and crowned his son Edward III. The king's campaign to force the barons to submit had been ultimately unsuccessful.

EDWARD III (1327–77)

The monarchy had taken a battering during the conflicts of the early 1320s, and Edward III aimed to revive its prestige. He spent most of his childhood training in knightly skills, and became king aged 14. A soldier at heart, with military glory his main ambition, Edward led the country into the Hundred Years' War with France. On the domestic front, he made efforts to come to an accommodation with the barons. Yet clashes were almost inevitable owing to the expense of war with France and his desire to reinforce English control in Scotland (see pages 64–5). Unlike his father, though, Edward III had the skills to negotiate with Parliament, and important steps were taken in the development of collaboration between the monarchy and Parliament.

THE HOUSE OF COMMONS

In the 14th century, the knights and burgesses chosen to represent their shires and towns began to sit in their own chamber in Parliament, the House of Commons, separate from the House of Lords where the nobles and senior clergy held their debates. Most power was held by the Lords – members of the great noble families related to the monarch. The non-feudal merchant class had little influence at this point but, as feudalism declined, the Commons became more important, and over the following centuries, the balance of power shifted towards the Commons.

The king's desperate need for funds led to a continual tug of war between him and Parliament, which led to parliamentary control over taxation. During the 1340s and early 1350s, Parliament refused to make grants to the king until he had dealt with their grievances. For example, in 1340, Edward pushed Parliament to concede to a tax of a ninth of corn, wool and sheep to pay for the war in France. In return, he had to allow the tax collectors to be accountable to Parliament and agree to let Parliament elect treasurers to oversee the spending of the tax revenues. For him, it was key to pursue the war in France, and if it was necessary to give up some power to Parliament to do this, then so be it. A few years later, the continental struggle started to go better, with the victories at Crécy and Calais, and the king found it easier to justify his demands for funds. Edward was able to prosecute his war, but a precedent of parliamentary supervision had been established.

THE BLACK DEATH

From 1347 to 1351, the Black Death ravaged Europe, hitting England in 1348 and then Scotland and Ireland in 1350. A virulent form of bubonic plague, it killed an estimated 40 per cent of the population (somewhere between 50 and 100 million people) – a human catastrophe. The plague, which originated in central Asia and was carried along land and sea trade routes by rat fleas, caused economic devastation. Lands were left uncultivated, wool production plummeted, and overseas trade collapsed. For the survivors, the effects on society were enormous. Feudal control collapsed, and serfs became free labourers, no longer beholden to their landlord.

The royal family had fled London and survived. At this

THE GREAT PLAGUE

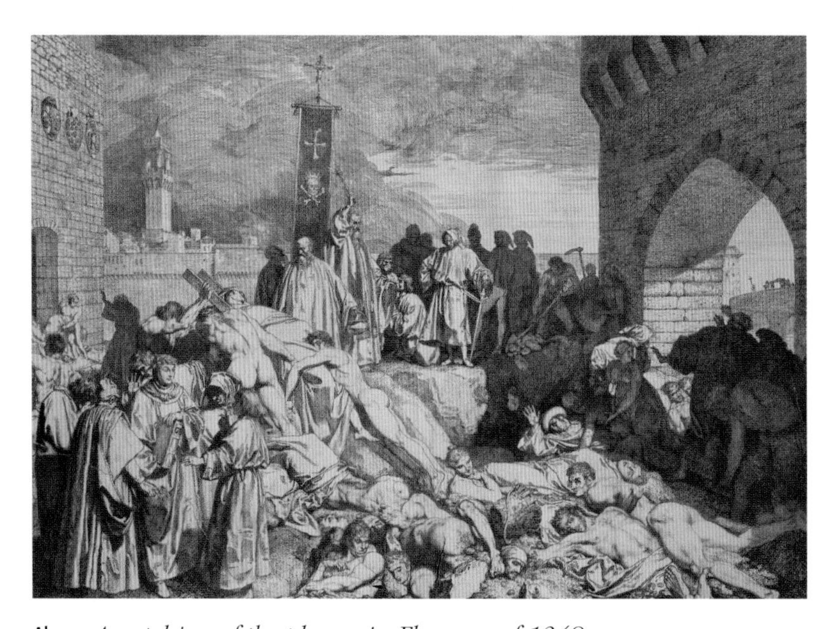

Above: *An etching of the plague in Florence of 1348.*

The Italian writer Giovanni Boccaccio survived the plague in Florence, Italy in 1348. He described the horror of catching the disease:

> *In men and women alike, at the beginning of the malady, certain swellings, either on the groin or under the armpits: waxed to the bigness of a common apple, others to the size of an egg, some more and some less, and these the vulgar named plague-boils.*

The swellings, called buboes, first appeared red-coloured and soon turned black, hence the name 'black death'. Boccaccio also outlined its extraordinarily infectious nature, which helped to account for the high death rate:

> *To speak to or go near the sick brought infection and a common death to the living; and moreover, to touch the clothes or anything else the sick had touched or worn gave the disease to the person touching.*[4]

time of crisis, the king worked with Parliament to try to restore order. Parliament introduced new laws to stop labourers and artisans demanding higher wages because of the severe labour shortage. In 1351, the Statute of Labourers stated, 'The old wages and no more shall be given to servants… If any take more Wages than were wont to be paid he shall be committed to Gaol.'[5] The statute proved futile – the workers were in an extremely strong bargaining position – but the nobles appreciated the king's support for their cause.

Following the shockwaves of the Black Death, trade gradually recovered, and a boom in the wool trade saw merchants making profits again. While the plague was disastrous for the landlords' interests, it was greatly beneficial for the merchants and marked an increase in their power.

Above: *John of Gaunt (left), the third of Edward III's five sons, was an influential figure during his father's reign.*

THE 'GOOD PARLIAMENT'

Political crisis dominated the latter years of Edward's reign. The renewal of the war with France plunged finances into a parlous state. The so-called 'Good Parliament' of 1376 attacked the high level of taxes, and the Commons criticized the King's courtiers and advisers for their corrupt practices. The charges were heard before the Lords, who banished Alice Perrers, the King's mistress, from the household for non-payment of money she had 'borrowed' from the royal coffers, and stripped the accused courtiers, William Latimer, Richard Lyons, John Neville, of office – the first impeachments in history. However, Edward's son John of Gaunt (who presided over Parliament on the now sick and elderly king's behalf) forced a reversal of the concessions by declaring the Good Parliament unconstitutional. Royal will still prevailed.

Richard II (1377–99)

Richard was the second son of Edward, Prince of Wales, the heir to Edward III's throne. Yet Richard's elder brother died in 1371 and his father passed away in 1376, leaving the succession to him. Richard II came to the throne aged 10, under a cloud of resentment at high taxation. With ongoing conflict with France and the attempt to dominate Ireland, the power struggle between the Crown and Parliament over finances continued; Richard was less successful than Edward III at negotiating with the nobles. Contemporaries and modern historians alike have judged Richard as tyrannical, based on his behaviour during the last two years of his reign, when he tried to push his royal authority too far and was deposed, imprisoned and possibly killed.

THE PEASANTS' REVOLT

From 1377 to 1380, Parliament introduced punitive poll taxes to pay for the war against France. The imposition led to one of the greatest upheavals of the Middle Ages in England – the Peasants' Revolt of 1381. Unlike previous levies, the poll taxes were highly regressive, foisted on working people as well as land and property owners. Many refused to pay. In 1381, enquiries were made into tax evasion, sparking widespread resistance in Essex, Kent, the Home Counties, East Anglia and Yorkshire. The resistance appeared to be coordinated. Led by an ex-soldier and now blacksmith from Maidstone, Walter 'Wat' Tyler, up to 100,000 agricultural workers marched to London in protest. It was the first widespread popular rebellion in English history.

Left: *Richard II in his coronation robes holding the orb and sceptre of office.*

Above: *Richard II meets with Wat Tyler, the leader of the Peasants' Revolt, in this 14th-century manuscript illustration.*

The government was unsure how to react. It was probably Richard's advisers and his mother who advised a meeting between the 14-year-old king and the rebels – a brave move for the young monarch. At the meeting, held on 14 June at Mile End, just outside London, Richard promised cheap land and free trade, and agreed to the abolition of serfdom. Emboldened by the king's concession, Wat Tyler made more radical demands the following day at another meeting with the king, this time just outside the city walls, at Smithfield. He demanded the removal of feudal lordship and the disestablishment of the Church. But this time, Tyler had gone too far and the Mayor of London, angered at the blacksmith's attitude towards the king, drew his dagger and stabbed Tyler in the neck. His supporters took the badly wounded Tyler to St Bartholemew's Hospital. At the mayor's orders, he was dragged from the hospital, taken back to Smithfield and beheaded. Tyler's murder marked the end of the revolt and the start of government suppression. Soldiers pursued the rebels throughout the Home Counties and many of them were hunted down and executed.

Despite its apparent failure and the fact that the king backtracked on all his promises, the revolt did make a difference. A revised poll tax in 1382 was imposed only on landowners to avoid further rebellion. Also, the Commons argued strongly that 'the king should live of his own' – on income from his properties and hereditary rights. Only in exceptional reasons should he raise customs duties and levies from Parliament. This was a significant attempt to reduce the power of the monarchy.

TYLER'S DEMANDS

The contemporary *Anonimalle Chronicle* described Wat Tyler's sweeping demands to the king:

> *There should be equality among all people save only the King, and that the goods of Holy Church should not remain in the hands of the religious, nor of parsons and vicars, and other churchmen; but that clergy already in possession should have a sufficient sustenance from the endowments, and the rest of the goods should be divided among the people of the parish. And he demanded that there should be only one bishop in England and only one prelate, and all the lands and tenements now held by them should be confiscated, and divided among the commons, only reserving for them a reasonable sustenance.*[6]

Above: *A 19th-century illustration shows the Lords Appellant confronting Richard II.*

PRESSURE FROM PARLIAMENT

The vexing issue of taxation also led to power struggles between the king and Parliament and between the king and his powerful opponents. In the mid-1380s, Richard bestowed several new noble titles, giving vast sums of funds to a few individuals, which Parliament deemed to be extravagant. The tensions led to crisis when the Royal Chancellor Michael de la Pole demanded a huge tax in 1386 to pay for coastal defences against an anticipated French invasion of England. Parliament refused to implement the tax and called for De la Pole to resign. Richard was forced to give way and replace his chancellor.

The following year, a group of five nobles named the Lords Appellant rebelled against the king and tried to seize power. They occupied London and set up the Merciless Parliament, subsequently purging the court and executing two of the king's main allies. By 1389, after two years of struggle between the Appellants and the king's supporters, Appellant power had receded, and Richard resumed his role as undisputed head of government. He promised to reduce taxation and include a wider circle of nobles in government.

ASSERTING ROYAL POWER

For a few years, Richard kept his promises, but he also reaffirmed his authority, insisting on new royal rituals akin to the ideals of kingship at the French court. He demanded to be called 'Your Highness' or 'Your Majesty' rather than 'My Lord' as previously, and he now wore his crown in Westminster Hall. Richard was also determined to restore the domination of the English lordship over Ireland. In 1394, he took an army of 5,000 to Ireland to crush the Irish resistance. Although the mission was successful, the Duke of Gloucester apparently declared that Ireland was 'a land neither of conquest nor of profit', and indeed, the victory proved ephemeral.[7]

From 1397, the king's behaviour shifted from assertive to tyrannical. He imprisoned, exiled or executed senior Appellants to prevent a reoccurrence of a nobles' rebellion; one of those banished was Henry Bolingbroke, the son of John of Gaunt, Duke of Lancaster. Richard used threats against Parliament to get his way: when Parliament convened, the king surrounded it with 200 archers to terrorize the members into doing his bidding. Parliament voted to give the king all the money he needed, and laws were introduced that defined most forms of opposition to the king as treason.

REVOLT

This assertion of royal power went too far. In 1399, the exiled Bolingbroke returned to England with his followers to recover his Lancastrian estates, and thousands joined his army. At the time, Richard was in Ireland, quelling a rebellion. When he came back, many of his soldiers deserted to Bolingbroke. The king sued for peace, surrendered and agreed to abdicate if his life was spared. He was the second Plantagenet deposed by Parliament. This time, Parliament appointed a king who was not the next in line to the throne. Bolingbroke became Henry IV, the first Lancastrian king. Richard was imprisoned, and the following year, which witnessed a rebellion in his favour, the first 'Royal Highness' lost his life in mysterious circumstances, possibly dying by his own hand.

Below: *Richard II surrenders to Henry Bolingbroke at Flint Castle.*

CHAPTER 7

THE HOUSES OF LANCASTER AND YORK 1399–1485

With no clear rules, succession to the throne was determined by force. The 15th-century monarchy was dominated by the Wars of the Roses between the houses of Lancaster and York, two branches of the Plantagenets. Yet this period of strife was probably no worse than the civil wars of the mid-13th century. To finance their military ventures, kings had to negotiate with Parliament, which increasingly demanded oversight of royal expenditure.

THE HOUSES OF LANCASTER AND YORK

Lancaster

Henry IV (1399–1413)
|
Henry V (1413–22)
|
Henry VI (1422–61 and 1470–71; King of France 1432–53)

York

Edward IV (1461–70)

Lancaster

Henry VI (1470–71)

York

Edward IV (1471–83)
|
Edward V (1483)
|
Richard III (1483–85)

HENRY IV, HOUSE OF LANCASTER (1399–1413)

I Henry of Lancastre chalenge this rewme of Yngland, and the corone with all the membres and the appurtenances, als I that am disendit be right lyne of the Blode comyng fro the gude lorde Kyng Henry therde, and thorgh that ryght that God of his grace hath sent me, with helpe of my Kyn and of my Frendes to recover it. (Source: J. Strachey, 1766–77)[1]

Pious in his personal life and well-educated, with a particular interest in the application of moral principles, Henry IV apparently saw no ethical problem in usurping the Crown from Richard II. To justify his accession, he claimed descent from Henry III and an ability to rescue the monarchy from the chaos of Richard's reign. Many at home and abroad, including Charles VI of France, did not recognize his claim, and he spent the early part of his reign fighting on several fronts. More accommodating than his predecessor, Henry was prepared to debate and negotiate with Parliament to reach agreement; since the relationship between the monarchy and Parliament was as yet undefined in law, compromise was the key to effective rule. The king retained the power to select his advisers and ministers, but Parliament had the right to oversee his activities.

Henry fought off challenges in Wales, Scotland and France simultaneously. In 1400, Owain Glyndwr rebelled against English

rule (see page 38) and the Scots made incursions into northern England. Meanwhile, the French attacked English-controlled territory in northern France and raided the southern English coast, while England counter-raided in northern France. The king dealt forcefully with several rebellions at home too, suppressing uprisings in 1403 and 1408.

Above: *The coronation of Henry IV at Westminster Abbey. He was the first monarch to make a speech in English at his coronation – previously the official language of the court had been French.*

PARLIAMENTARY POWERS GROW

As well as extracting Parliamentary grants for his military ventures, Henry had extravagant tastes at court. Parliament accused the king of poor financial management and demanded controls over royal spending. This came to a head in 1406, when Parliament stated that it would proffer a new grant only if it could audit its 1404 grant; the king reluctantly agreed. In 1406, a special Council took over management of the Crown's finances, and by 1409, the king's financial problems had been resolved. Allowing Parliament to keep an eye on his spending proved beneficial for the king. Despite factionalism at court during the last six years of his reign, as Henry's eldest son Prince Henry demanded a bigger role in government, the underlying strength of the regime was maintained until the king's death from illness in March 1413.

HENRY V, HOUSE OF LANCASTER (1413–22)

A man of action, Henry V is mainly remembered for his victory in France. Yet although primarily a warrior king, he maintained firm control over his realm and made England one of the strongest kingdoms in Europe. While away on his frequent trips to France, Henry left the government in the capable hands of Councils run efficiently by his brothers. Parliament did not feel the need to step in, and Henry avoided the conflict with Parliament which afflicted his predecessors. On the negative side, the king treated his enemies ruthlessly, and prioritized a campaign in France which was of arguable benefit to Britain.

Motivated to serve God and to secure the Church's support, Henry founded three monasteries and defended the established religious order from opposition through his merciless repression of the Lollard sect. Following John Wycliffe's teachings, the Lollards stressed the importance of Scripture and preaching, and opposed the papacy, arguing it had no basis in the Bible. Henry IV had been determined to stamp out this heresy and in 1401 had approved a law that permitted the burning of heretics at the stake. Following a Lollard protest in 1414, around 300 members were arrested, 38 of whom were executed for treason. The failed rising was used as an excuse to repress Lollardy, and the movement went underground.

OBSESSION WITH FRANCE

Henry V was fixated on the French throne, claiming the title King of France through his great-grandfather Edward III. However, negotiations were not successful, and in April 1415 the English Parliament granted him a 'double subsidy' to finance the renewal of the Hundred Years' War. In August, Henry launched a campaign that would last until his death. His forces triumphed at the Battle of Agincourt

HOTSPUR'S REBELLION, 1403

Henry 'Hotspur' Percy and his father had supported Henry's usurpation and were handsomely rewarded with land in northern England and Wales. They harried the Scots and roundly defeated them in Durham in 1402. But when the king delayed repaying Percy's war expenses, Percy turned against him; in 1403, he led an uprising, calling on support in Cheshire and Wales and falsely claiming that Richard II still lived. King Henry was victorious against the rebels at the Battle of Shrewsbury, and Hotspur died on the battlefield.

Above: *A modern illustration of Henry Hotspur at the Battle of Shrewsbury in 1403.*

Opposite: *A 16th-century portrait of Henry V. He was renowned for his military prowess and preferred the battlefield to the court room.*

THE BATTLE OF AGINCOURT, 1415

Left: *A contemporary illustration of the Battle of Agincourt, 1415, at which Henry V personally led the English forces to victory.*

The English had repulsed the main French assault, the longbowmen particularly effective against the heavily armoured French men-at-arms in the confined space of the muddy battlefield. The French suffered heavy casualties, and many hundreds of others were taken prisoner. When Henry heard that French reinforcements were drawing near, he worried that those captured soldiers, who now outnumbered their captors, might grab the weapons that lay discarded on the battlefield and join in the fighting again. In order to prevent this, he ordered his knights to kill all their prisoners rather than ransom them later. A Flemish boy, Jehan de Wavrin, whose father and brother died fighting with the French, witnessed King Henry's mercilessness:

> *... he appointed a gentleman with two hundred archers whom he commanded to go through the host and kill all the prisoners, whoever they might be. This esquire, without delay or objection, fulfilled the command of his sovereign lord, which was a most pitiable thing, for in cold blood all the nobility of France was beheaded and inhumanly cut to pieces.*[2]

The battle was disastrous for the French. Led by constable Charles I d'Albret, around 6,000 of the total army of 20,000 to 30,000 soldiers were killed, while King Henry lost fewer than 450 fighters. The poor tactics of the French army, combined with Henry's successful albeit ruthless leadership, led to English victory.

on 25 October 1415, despite the overwhelming numerical superiority of the French army. His military successes continued, and in 1420 he secured the Treaty of Troyes, by which he would marry Catherine, the daughter of Charles VI of France and become King of France after Charles' death. Henry was never able to take advantage of his victory; he died, at only 36, supposedly of dysentery, in 1422.

HENRY VI, HOUSE OF LANCASTER (1422–61 AND 1470–71)

Henry VI inherited the throne as a baby and took on full royal responsibilities aged just 16. From 1437, he wore his crown in public and henceforth all matters of 'grete weght and charge' were referred to him.[3] This young man was faced with the daunting inheritance of a dual monarchy – he was king of both England and France – but proved incapable of meeting the challenge. With a character unsuited to political or military leadership, he also suffered from mental-health problems in later years. His reign was marked by losses in France, weak administration at home and rebellions. Historians see his personality as one of the causes of the Wars of the Roses.

Henry was a poor administrator and under his auspices, public order declined. With a feeble monarchy, others stepped in to fill the power vacuum. The most influential adviser of the 1430s–40s was William de la Pole, Earl of Suffolk; as Henry's steward he reaped much in personal gain, vastly increasing the size of the royal household and siphoning off funds for himself and his circle. The war in France to maintain control of Normandy depleted the royal coffers further. Both the Dauphin

Below: *Henry VI is crowned king of France in 1432 in Notre Dame cathedral, Paris.*

and the citizen leader Joan of Arc had successes fighting England, and in 1450 Henry lost Normandy; by 1453, only Calais remained under English rule. The Hundred Years' War was over.

THE WARS OF THE ROSES

In 1453, Henry's mental health collapsed, and Richard of York was appointed protector of the realm. Although the king recovered at the end of 1454 and took charge again, his health remained impaired and he was unable to cope with the impending conflict.

A dynastic struggle erupted between the Houses of York and Lancaster in 1455, leading to a series of wars. In 1460, Yorkist leader Richard of York brazenly claimed Henry's throne for himself. To meet the threat, the Lancastrians fought, defeated and killed Richard at the Battle of Wakefield. Edward IV, heir of Richard of York, continued his father's mission and seized the throne in 1461. King Henry's life was spared, and his queen, Margaret of Anjou, hurried the family to safety in Scotland. She adopted the role of defending her husband's throne and the Lancastrian cause, commanding an army to fight from a base in Northumberland. When after three years her mission eventually failed, she sought refuge in France. Margaret's fortunes changed in 1470 when Edward's right-hand man, the Earl of Warwick, switched sides and joined forces with her to depose Edward and reinstate Henry. However, the restoration was brief; Edward regained the throne the following year after defeating the Lancastrians at the Battle of Tewkesbury. This time, the ousted king was imprisoned and died in the Tower of London – officially from 'melancholy', but more likely killed on Edward's orders.

Despite his lack of leadership abilities, Henry VI was the third-longest reigning monarch since 1066. His interest in education led to his foundation of Eton College and King's College, Cambridge, both of which still flourish today. Yet he remains best known for his legacy of civil war.

Opposite: *The chapel of King's College, Cambridge. The college was founded by Henry VI on 12 February 1441.*

Left: *A late-15th-century miniature of Joan of Arc.*

Below: *The Earl of Warwick begs for pardon from Margaret of Anjou.*

THE BATTLE OF WAKEFIELD

Margaret of Anjou, commanding Lancastrian forces of around 15,000 soldiers, crushed the smaller Yorkist army of 4,000 at the Battle of Wakefield. An eyewitness described how the Yorkists were surrounded: 'When [Richard of York] was in the plain ground between his castle and the town of Wakefield, he was environed on every side, like a fish in a net or a deer in a buckstall [a snare for trapping deer].'[4] The would-be usurper was killed in battle.

THE KING'S CONTRADICTIONS

The *Crowland Chronicle*, written in 1483, expresses the contradictions of King Edward IV's behaviour. Although enjoying hedonistic pastimes, he did not neglect his royal duties and had strong personal authority. Men of the kingdom:

> *wondered that a man of such corpulence, and so fond of boon companionship, vanities, debauchery, extravagance, and sensual enjoyments, should have had a memory so retentive, in all respects, that the names and estates used to recur to him, just as though he had been in the habit of seeing them daily, of nearly all the persons dispersed throughout the counties of this kingdom.*[5]

Above: *A miniature depicting the Battle of Tewkesbury of 1471. It was a decisive battle in the Wars of the Roses.*

EDWARD IV, HOUSE OF YORK (1461–83, EXCEPT 1470–71)

Once secure on the throne, Edward enjoyed creature comforts and a luxurious lifestyle at court, the splendour of his surroundings reflecting his political power. From 1471, the Yorkists were firmly in control. Most prominent Lancastrians had been killed, and the survivors made peace with the regime. The European economic recovery also contributed greatly to the success of Edward's reign.

Edward ruled with a strong hand, relying on his own considerable military acumen as well as on close advisors and trusted noble relatives to exercise power in the provinces and vigilance against rebellion. He took personal control of the judicial system, reviving the old custom of sitting in person to enforce justice. The king travelled around the country to hear petitions and oversee administration by his nobles and thus restored confidence in the judicial system.

PEACE AND PROSPERITY

During the early 1470s, the king prepared to invade France to recover territory lost by his predecessor, believing that fighting a common enemy would unite the English. In 1475, he travelled to France with a large army to exert pressure on the French King Louis XI. But Louis opted not to fight, offering instead to pay Edward 50,000 gold crowns a year to return to England (although in the event, he only paid the fee sporadically) and not to pursue his claim to the French throne. A commercial treaty was agreed, and peace prevailed until the end of Edward's reign.

Opposite: *A 16th-century portrait of King Edward IV. This painting was one of a series of royal portraits commissioned during the reign of Henry VIII.*

European economies were recovering during this period; peace with France and a stable regime helped the British economy to thrive too. Edward encouraged commercial treaties with France and the Hanseatic League (a trading guild in Northern Europe) as well as the Mediterranean states. Trade with other European countries, such as Spain, also expanded. The developing merchant class gave their support to the king for assisting their activities. Edward himself traded in wool to revive his personal income so he could 'live of his own.' He used the profits from the Crown estates to pay the costs of administering the country. The king therefore had no need to ask Parliament for subsidies, avoiding conflict over taxation.

Edward died unexpectedly, aged 41, without leaving clear instructions about an heir; his son Edward was only 12. On his deathbed, he named his brother Richard as his inheritor, but his wishes were not set down in writing. His death, like that of Henry VI, is shrouded in mystery. Some contemporary chroniclers attributed it to illness, others his excessive indulgence in food and drink. Whatever the reason, having achieved stability in his reign, he bequeathed a succession crisis on his death.

Above: *A 15th-century manuscript illustration of merchants trading in France. Edward IV negotiated a commercial treaty with Burgundy in 1468 for diplomatic as much as financial reasons.*

EDWARD V, HOUSE OF YORK (1483)

Edward's eldest son, the 12-year-old King Edward V, ruled for just a few months from April to June 1483 before being deposed, incarcerated and killed. Edward's protector was his uncle Richard, brother of the deceased Edward IV. Richard, the Duke of Gloucester, was suspicious that the Woodvilles, the family of Edward's mother Elizabeth, were planning to seize power. As Edward was travelling to London for his coronation, Richard intercepted him at Stoney Stratford in Buckinghamshire and bundled the boy into the Tower of London, where he was soon joined by his brother. Richard challenged Edward's right to the throne, declaring he was illegitimate because his father had made a marriage contract with Lady Eleanor Butler before marrying Elizabeth Woodville, and usurped the crown, proclaiming himself Richard III. The princes were never seen or heard from again. Richard was suspected of having them murdered; 200 years later, in 1674, two children's skeletons were discovered by workmen demolishing a staircase in the White Tower. The record of John Knight, King Charles II's principal surgeon, indicates that they belonged to the young princes.

Below: *Edward V with his parents, Edward IV and Elizabeth Woodville, as portrayed in the* Dictes and Sayings of Philosophers *(1477).*

RICARDVS .RIX.
ANGLYA , III

RICHARD III, HOUSE OF YORK (1483–85)

Opposite: *A portrait of Richard III. Richard had spent much of the decade before his accession to the throne in the north of England, fighting off Scottish incursions.*

He is infamous for the alleged murder of his nephews to usurp the throne, and infighting within the Yorkist family led to the downfall of Richard and his dynasty.

At first, Richard had indicated his intentions to govern well and maintain law and order, but his machinations to seize the throne alienated the nobles from the start and they lacked confidence in him. Opponents within the House of York rebelled against the new king soon after his accession, led by the Duke of Buckingham, acting in the name of the Lancastrian claimant Henry Tudor. Two years later, Henry Tudor himself arrived in Wales with an army from France. His forces clashed with Richard's Yorkist army at the Battle of Bosworth Field in 1485. During the battle, Richard received intelligence that Henry Tudor had become isolated from his troops and led a small group in for the kill. Waiting in the wings were the uncommitted forces of Lord Thomas Stanley, which now weighed in to defend Henry and attack Richard. The king became stuck in marshy ground, had to dismount and faced his enemies on foot, preferring to die rather than face capture. He met his death on the battlefield. The way was open for the beginning of a new dynasty: the Tudors.

ROYAL REMAINS

Richard had no funeral ceremony, and no one knew the exact location of his burial until 2012, when archaeologists discovered a skeleton in a Leicester car park exhibiting scoliosis and battle injuries. A contemporary Welsh poem in praise of Rhys ap Tomas, who supported Henry Tudor's army, described Richard's death:

... King Henry won the day
through the strength of our master
killing Englishmen, capable hand,
killing the boar, he shaved his head... [7]

The poet's description matched the injuries on the skeleton – the top of the skull had indeed been sliced off. In 2013, genetic tests proved that the remains belonged to the last Yorkist monarch.

Above: *The new tomb of Richard III in Leicester Cathedral.*

RICHARD'S REPUTATION

Stories subsequently proliferated about Richard, implying that he was a hunchback and evil by nature. It is true that he had scoliosis, but the hunchback and murdering instincts were exaggerated later by Tudor propaganda to justify the dynasty's takeover from the Yorkists.[8] In the 20th century, some historians attempted to rehabilitate Richard III's reputation. They pointed to his attempts to improve the administration of justice, his piety and his popularity in the north of England. Nowadays, most historians consider that this revised view of Richard is overstated. They believe that his claim to throne was dubious and that he acted outside the law, murdering his nephews and other opponents without trial.[9]

CHAPTER 8

THE TUDORS 1485–1603

The ferocious rivalry of the Houses of York and Lancaster was over, to be replaced by a new civil conflict over religion. Like a butterfly effect, the desire of Henry VIII for a divorce prompted far reaching changes: the English Reformation and decades of struggle between Catholics and Protestants. The religious wrangling did not prevent economic development though. An era of European exploration began in Tudor times, bringing riches from trade and exploitation, and new ideas; the monarchy benefited greatly from this period of prosperity. The Tudors did not rule alone – they had to recognize the importance of Parliament in running the country and relied on talented public servants. Yet the most dynamic king and queen, Henry VIII and Elizabeth I, had a substantial personal impact on politics, economics and society.

HENRY VII (1485–1509)

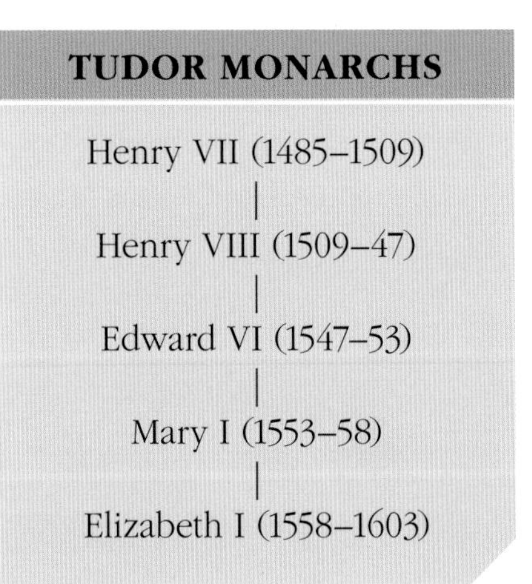
TUDOR MONARCHS

Henry VII (1485–1509)
|
Henry VIII (1509–47)
|
Edward VI (1547–53)
|
Mary I (1553–58)
|
Elizabeth I (1558–1603)

Henry VII ended the War of the Roses, marrying Elizabeth of York to unite the houses of Lancaster and York and founding the Tudor dynasty. To stamp his authority on the land after three decades of civil war, he ruled harshly. Was his assertion of royal authority necessary to stabilize the country or did his tyrannical tendencies have a destabilizing effect? Historians today give a mixed verdict on the success of Henry's rule.

SECURING STABILITY

Henry's throne certainly remained insecure, and there were several Yorkist plots against him. One pretender was Perkin Warbeck. The son of a boatman from Tournai, Belgium, Warbeck was persuaded in 1491 to pretend that he was Richard, Duke of York (the younger of the princes in the Tower), who had somehow escaped from the Tower of London. By 1493, the king had uncovered the plot and brought treason trials against Warbeck's associates. When Warbeck landed with a force of 300 men in Kent in 1495, he and his followers were captured. The Englishmen among them were hanged for treason, while the pretender himself was eventually executed in 1499. Henry's message to his enemies was clear.

Henry acted equally severely towards perceived enemies at home. Suspicious of the nobles, he saw them as a potential threat and imprisoned, exiled or executed

Opposite: *A contemporary portrait of Henry VII.*

SPIES AND MOLES

Historian Francis Bacon (1561–1626) justified Henry's use of spies to root out conspiracies hatched by treacherous 'moles' to bring pretenders to the throne:

> *As for his secret spials [spies] which he did employ both at home and abroad, by them to discover what practices and conspiracies were against him; surely his case required it; he had such moles perpetually working and casting to undermine him. Neither can it be reprehended; for if spials be lawful against lawful enemies, much more against conspirators and traitors.*[1]

Above: *Perkin Warbeck is paraded through the streets of London following his capture. He later confessed to being born in Tournai in modern-day Belgium.*

potential claimants to the throne. To keep the nobility under his control, he fined them for failing to pay archaic feudal obligations. Henry's security policy was successful and he maintained internal stability, although his methods were unpopular.

ECONOMIC EXPLOITATION

Henry's economic policy was equally disliked. Rather than relying on parliamentary taxation, he increased customs duties and exploited feudal rights to the maximum, taking the revenues collected from Crown lands by the sheriffs and seizing income from wardships (whereby the king took control of land when a minor inherited it, oversaw it and took the revenue until that minor came of age). He increased the Crown's revenue from an average of £52,000 a year to £142,000 by the end of his reign. He was no miser, though. The king was extravagant at court, refurbishing his royal palaces and decorating them richly with tapestries, jewels and plate to demonstrate the magnificence of his kingship and the security of his position.

Above: *An 18th-century print of Richmond Palace, based on an earlier drawing. Little now remains of the palace, as it was demolished soon after the execution of Charles I in 1649.*

A MIXED LEGACY

Henry successfully established a new dynasty, defeating his opponents, providing heirs to the succession and achieving financial stability. Yet he ruled through fear and was not loved by his subjects. In his funeral sermon for the king, Priest John Fisher gives an indication of this duality:

'… his mighty power was dread everywhere, not only within his realm but without also … his land many a day in peace and tranquillity, his prosperity in battle against his enemies was marvellous, his dealing in time of perils and dangers was cold and sober with great hardiness.'[2]

HENRY VIII (1509–47)

… rarely, if ever, have the unawareness and irresponsibility of a king proved more costly of the material benefit of his people.
(Historian Jack Scarisbrick)[3]

Below: *A contemporary portrait of Cardinal Thomas Wolsey. Wolsey was Henry VIII's right-hand man until his failure to convince the pope to annul the marriage between the king and Catherine of Aragon.*

One of the strongest of Britain's monarchs, Henry VIII was also one of the least popular. He is best known for his six wives and the break with the Catholic Church. The English Church and the state were united, and the property of the former was transferred to the latter, a transition that marked the beginning of the Protestant Reformation in Britain. Henry's actions also established the right of Parliament to be involved in making changes to the country's religion and the dynasty. The outcome of Henry's driving ambition for an heir had unintended consequences that irrevocably changed the relationship between the state and the Church.

Henry VIII started his reign from a strong position: the economy was healthy and his father had accrued much wealth for the Crown. His policy was to attract nobles to court and turn them into courtiers so they would become allies rather than opponents – a successful although expensive strategy. For the first 20 years of his reign, Henry relied on Thomas Wolsey to direct his policies; Wolsey became

Above: *The entrance to Hampton Court Palace. Wolsey gave the palace to Henry VIII as a gift to help regain the monarch's favour.*

Opposite: *A portrait of Henry VIII by Hans Holbein the Younger, produced between 1537 and 1547. The original commission was a mural in Whitehall Palace and included his wife at the time, Jane Seymour, but only copies of the section showing the king have survived.*

the king's principal royal minister from 1515 and power was increasingly concentrated in his hands. Wolsey used the Court of Star Chamber (an instrument of the king's prerogative, unbound by common law or the use of juries) to prosecute slander, fraud and various other offences against the king. As Cardinal from 1515, he also governed the Church.

DIVORCE FROM CATHERINE AND ROME

The succession crisis became the defining issue of Henry's reign. Shortly after his accession, he had married his brother's widow, Catherine of Aragon, but by the 1520s, the couple still only had a daughter, Princess Mary. Henry began to see their failure to produce a male heir as a punishment for marrying his brother's wife, which is prohibited in the Bible. Not since Boudicca in the 1st century had any part of England been ruled by a queen, and Henry did not want to risk leaving the Crown to a female heir. He feared it would lead to dispute, a male claimant seizing the throne and ending the Tudor dynasty, or a foreign power gaining control by marrying his daughter. Henry therefore asked the Pope to annul his marriage. Previous monarchs had been granted a divorce and, in normal circumstances, it would have been acceptable. Yet Charles V of France was now the ruler of Italy. Catherine of Aragon was Charles's aunt, and the Pope could not afford to move against him. Wolsey was unable to secure the Pope's agreement for Henry's divorce, so Henry dismissed his faithful minister.

WAR WITH FRANCE

Like many of his predecessors, Henry fought to reclaim English lands in France. But France had become richer and more powerful and had a strong monarch in Louis XII. In 1518, after five years of war, Henry had spent his father's inheritance and decided to make peace, marrying his sister Mary to the King of France and signing the Treaty of Universal Amity. Yet Henry would return to war in the 1540s, invading France in 1542 and securing Boulogne, and renewing the age-old conflict with Scotland (see page 125).

Above: *A painting from 1545 of the meeting between Henry VIII and Francis I at the Field of the Cloth of Gold in northern France in June 1520. The lavish event marked the beginning of amicable relations between the two powers which lasted more than 20 years.*

Opposite: *Catherine of Aragon, as depicted in a portrait from 1530. She supported the work of leading humanist intellectuals, including Thomas More and Erasmus.*

Henry changed tack, pushing through legal changes to reduce papal power in England. In 1531, the king persuaded the clergy to recognize him as Supreme Head of the Church of England 'as far as the law of Christ allows'. He forced them to allow him a veto over ecclesiastical legislation. Loyal to the Catholic Church, Thomas More now resigned as Lord Chancellor. Thomas Cromwell became Henry's right-hand man; as his chief advisor from 1532, he engineered the split from the Church in Rome, using the power of Parliament to help Henry to secure a divorce without the Pope's involvement. For this, he needed a cooperative Archbishop of Canterbury; Thomas

NNA BOLINA VXOR
HENRI OCTA

Opposite: *Anne Boleyn, Henry VIII's second wife. She was beheaded in 1536 for high treason.*

Right: *Hans Holbein's portrait of Thomas Cromwell, 1532–3. He was one of the leading figures of the English Reformation.*

'THE NUN OF KENT'

Young servant Elizabeth Barton, nicknamed 'The Nun of Kent', claimed she received holy visions urging King Henry not to divorce Catherine of Aragon, and inspired opposition to his plan to marry Anne Boleyn. In 1532, Barton confronted the king directly as he passed through Canterbury:

> *Henry, forsake Anne Boleyn and take back your wife Catherine… If you neglect these things, you shall not be King longer than a month, and in God's eyes you will not be so even for an hour. You shall die the death of a villain, and Mary, the daughter of Catherine, shall wear your crown.*[4]

Deemed a treacherous threat, Barton was arrested, made to confess to inventing her prophecies and then executed. It has never been proved whether or not her confession was genuine, but she undoubtedly articulated the concerns of many people about the king's divorce.

Cranmer was appointed in 1532. Henry secretly married Anne Boleyn (the sister of one of his many mistresses and Catherine's lady-in-waiting, Mary) in January 1533. In May, Cranmer declared Henry's first marriage invalid, and Anne Boleyn was crowned queen one week later. Most people in the country disapproved of the union and sympathized with the rejected Queen Catherine.

In retaliation for his actions, the Pope excommunicated Henry. The king sought a legal break from Rome, declaring that England was now an empire with one head; the excommunication was therefore invalid because the Pope no longer held authority over

Above: *A 19th-century painting of Sir Thomas More meeting his daughter after he has been condemned to death.*

England. The 1534 Act of Supremacy made Henry Supreme Head of the Church of England, and it became treasonable to deny it. Thomas More refused to declare allegiance to Henry above the Church and gave up his life for principles; as he walked to the scaffold he stated that he would die 'in the faith and for the faith of the Catholic Church, the king's good servant and God's first'.[5]

RELIGIOUS REFORM

The king's political cause led to religious change throughout the country, although he had previously opposed reform of the Church and did not intend such developments. The break with Rome provided fertile ground for the ideas of Calvinism and Lutheranism to grow – chiefly that individuals enjoyed a direct relationship with God, with no need for the clergy as intermediates. A groundswell of anti-clericalism helped to launch the English Reformation.

Above: *A 19th-century engraving portraying the dissolution of the monasteries.*

DISSOLVING THE MONASTERIES

Another core element of the Reformation was the dissolution of the monasteries. Henry found it hard to 'live of his own'; with Wolsey's help, he had increased the Crown's revenue from taxation. He introduced a subsidy from Parliament in 1512, a wealth-based tax, and by the mid-1520s, about 90 per cent of rural and around two-thirds of town households had to pay it. The increasing burden of taxation led to disgruntlement. Although the ostensible reason for dissolving the monasteries was that they were corrupt, Henry had a clear economic incentive for the closure programme. In 1535 and 1536, 200 small monasteries were dissolved, followed by the large houses from 1538 to 1540. Their land, property and goods all went to the king, and revenues to the Crown doubled for a few years.

HENRY VIII'S WIVES

1 **Catherine of Aragon:** married 1509–33. Died 1536. Her daughter became Mary I (see image on page 100).
2 **Anne Boleyn:** married 1533–36; executed 1536. Her daughter became Elizabeth I (see image on page 102).
3 **Jane Seymour:** married 1536–7; died after giving birth. Her son became Edward VI.
4 **Anne of Cleves:** married Jan–July 1540; died 1557.
5 **Catherine Howard:** married 1540–42; beheaded 1542 for unproven revelations of adultery.
6 **Catherine Parr:** married 1543 and remained Henry's wife until his death in 1547.

Jane Seymour

Anne of Cleves

Catherine Howard

Catherine Parr

THE PILGRIMAGE OF GRACE

Surprisingly, Henry's Reformation did not cause widespread social unrest; the most serious challenge was the 1536 Pilgrimage of Grace in the north of England. The rebellion was sparked by financial, social and political grievances, including the dissolution of the religious houses, which had offered employment and charity. The movement called for the restoration of the abbeys. Henry indicated he would consider the protesters' complaints but instead endorsed a campaign of vengeance that resulted in more than 200 brutal executions. He wrote:

You shal in any wise cause suche dredfull execution to be doon upon a good nombre of thinhabitauntes of every towne, village and hamlet that have offended in this rebellion, aswell by hanging of them uppe in trees, as by the quartering of them and the setting of their heddes and quarters in every towne…[6]

Above: *An illustration showing the Pilgrimage of Grace of 1536. Approximately 40,000 people were involved in the uprising.*

DEFENDER OF THE FAITH?

Henry's separation of the English Church from the Church of Rome was for purely practical reasons. In 1521, he had written a best-selling book, *Defence of the Seven Sacraments,* attacking the ideas of Martin Luther which formed the basis of the Protestant Reformation, and offering his full support to the Catholic Church. In 1537, he explained that the circumstances were now different, so he had changed his mind: 'We princes wrote ourselves to be inferiors to popes; as long as we thought so we obeyed them as our superiors. Now we write not as we did.'[7]

SOCIAL TRANSFORMATION

The dissolution of the monasteries had a significant impact on landowning. The Crown gave away some of the newly acquired land in return for feudal knight service, and leased or sold a large part of it. Two-thirds of lords bought or were granted land. Most of the land from the monastic estates went to existing landowners and would never return to the Church.

The separation from the Catholic Church affected religious practice in England too. Christian worship officially changed: it was the end of the cult of saints, pilgrimage, the display of relics and the use of shrines. A new Bible in English was adopted. But it took time for the Church of England to become established, and the changes were contested. Following the king's death in 1547, the country remained divided between Protestants and Catholics, leading to conflict and martyrdom on both sides for decades to come.

Edward VI (1547–53)

The story of the boy king Edward VI's reign is mostly the story of his lord protectors, first his uncle Edward Seymour, the Duke of Somerset, and from 1549 John Dudley, the Earl of Warwick. Edward's protectors involved him in government but he did not exercise authority, and they pursued their own agendas. His reign was dominated by the Protestant Reformation. Cranmer's coronation speech declared that the king was Supreme Head of the Church by divine appointment: 'Your Majesty is God's Viceregent, and Christ's Vicar within your own Dominions'.[8]

Arguably, the young king, aged nine when he came to the throne, had some impact on religious change, since he was a fervent Protestant who approved of the Reformation. But it was the Duke of Somerset who set the Reformation in motion, and it was shaped by Archbishop Cranmer. In 1549, Cranmer introduced the Book of Common Prayer, a Protestant liturgy to replace the Catholic Mass, and English replaced Latin in services. Churches were transformed. Royal commissioners removed all religious imagery, statues and stained glass; candles disappeared, since ceremonies such as blessing candles at Candlemas were banned; decorated walls were white-washed. Churches became completely plain to avoid distractions and encourage the congregation to focus on God.

Below: *In this allegorical painting, the ailing Henry VIII lays in bed while Edward VI sits triumphant behind the defeated pope. To the left of Edward stands his trusted advisor Lord Seymour.*

Left: *An early 20th-century illustration of Kett's Rebellion of 1549. Robert Kett was a target of the rebels before he offered to join them.*

BANNED FESTIVITIES

In the austere new Protestant culture, many well-loved customs were banned, including mystery plays, holy-day pageants and dancing around the maypole. A pre-Christian tradition, the May Day festivities, with young people flirting and drinking as they danced around a tree or pole decorated with ribbons and flowers to celebrate the spring, were deemed un-Godly.

Above: *A 17th-century painting of the traditional dance around the maypole on May Day.*

RIOT AND REBELLION

The introduction of Cranmer's prayer book in 1549 sparked rebellion in Cornwall, Devon and Somerset. It began with petitioning, progressed to rioting, and a rebel army formed to attack the Crown's forces. In the same year, Kett's Rebellion erupted in Norfolk, sparked by social and economic injustices. The authorities brutally crushed these revolts, killing the resisters and hunting down rebel leaders.

FALL OF THE DUKE OF SOMERSET

Following the revolts, the gentry and nobility expressed their doubts about the leadership of Somerset, who had initially tried to bargain with the rebels. They feared negotiation would damage their interests. Somerset was also perceived as an arrogant man who made decisions without consultation. As historian David Loades notes, he 'appeared to be forgetting he was not the king'.[9] On the other hand, John Dudley, the Earl of Warwick, had proved his worth by quelling Kett's rebellion. Now in the ascendancy, he overthrew Somerset, and in 1550 became President of the Council and the king's protector. Warwick opted

Above: *Edward Seymour, the Duke of Somerset, who ruled as Lord Protector from 1547 to 1549.*

to end the war with France, mediating a treaty in 1550 to sell Boulogne back to France and for Edward to marry the French king's daughter. Somerset disapproved of the treaty and plotted to overthrow his successor. Realizing the threat from Somerset, Warwick had him arrested in 1551 and sent to the Tower, where he was executed in January 1552. Edward was no longer close to his uncle and former protector. His diary entry for the event merely stated: 'Today, the Duke of Somerset had his head cut off on Tower Hill.'[10]

Edward became ill in 1553. Henry VIII had decreed that if Edward died childless, the throne should go to his eldest sister Mary, daughter of Catherine of Aragon, and then to Princess Elizabeth. But when it became clear that Edward was dying, the Duke of Northumberland intervened to declare his daughter Jane Grey the successor to the throne. She was a Protestant and Edward was happy for her to

LADY JANE GREY

Lady Jane Grey (1537–54) married Lord Guildford Dudley in May 1553. His father, John, Duke of Northumberland, was one of Edward VI's most influential advisers. Northumberland persuaded the young king to nominate Jane, a Protestant, as his heir. Little more than a month later, Edward VI was dead. On 10 July 1553, the 15-year-old Jane was proclaimed Queen. Her reign lasted only nine days. Her coronation was supported by the Privy Council, but it soon became clear that the wider population preferred Mary. Dudley left London with an army two days into Jane's reign, to suppress the force Mary was raising. His forces soon melted away and the council abruptly withdrew its support from Jane. On 20 July, Jane was imprisoned in the Tower of London, and on 13 November she was found guilty of treason. On 12 February 1554 she was executed along with her husband.

Above: *Lady Jane Grey was queen for a mere nine days before she was deposed by Mary.*

succeed him. Yet Jane Grey's claim to the succession was considered distant; she was the great-granddaughter of Henry VII. Most people considered Mary, the daughter of Henry VIII and Catherine of Aragon, to be the rightful heir and Mary enjoyed widespread support. Thus Edward's last wishes were ignored.

MARY I (1553–58)

Nicknamed 'Bloody Mary' for her determination to restore the ascendancy of the Catholic Church, Queen Mary's religious policy fostered social division and intense persecution of Protestants. Yet it was popular with people who had never accepted religious change, dissent was mostly quashed, and Mary proved that a woman could rule in her own right. The restoration of Catholicism could not be consolidated in five years, however, and Mary had no Catholic heir to pursue her ambitions.

CATHOLICISM RETURNS

Immediately after her accession, Mary embarked on the restoration of Roman Catholicism. She abandoned the title of Supreme Head of the Church, returning the position to the Pope, and brought back Catholic bishops and monastic orders. Parish churches were redecorated, people said masses for the dead once more, and Mary introduced a new children's catechism (book of fundamental beliefs) and Book of Homilies (collection of authorized sermons). Her attempt to persuade the gentry who had bought monastic lands to return them proved a step too far though; they refused.

To enforce the changes, Mary reinstated the laws for punishing heretics: not following the faith of the monarch was decreed to be a

Opposite: *A 1544 portrait of Mary I. In the same year, a declaration stated that the authority of the monarch was the same whether the monarch was male or female.*

ANNO DNI
1544
ADI MARI
HE MOST
ING HENRI
DOVGHTER TO
VERTVOVS PRINC
THE EIGHT
HE AGE OF
XXVIII YERES

treasonous offence. Within three years, around 300 Protestants were burned at the stake, including Thomas Cranmer, the former Archbishop of Canterbury. (The latter could be seen as Mary's revenge for Cranmer annulling Henry VIII's marriage to her mother.) Several hundred Protestants from different levels of society fled the country as refugees.

Mary's eagerness to punish Protestants could be seen as counterproductive. It was mostly ordinary Protestants rather than prominent churchmen who went to the stake; committed to the new religion, they were prepared to die for their beliefs. In 1557, they were being 'burned in batches' and although the killings were supposed to act as a warning to others, there was sympathy for the victims. In London, Bishop Bonner argued for early-morning burnings before the crowds arrived, to avoid their hostility.

JOHN FOXE'S *BOOK OF MARTYRS*

Puritan preacher John Foxe detailed the martyrdom of English Protestants in his *Book of Martyrs*, with graphic descriptions and vivid illustrations of burnings to exemplify the faith and dignity of the victims. He described Archbishop Cranmer's execution in 1556 for promoting Protestantism:

> *… when the wood was kindled and the fire began to burn near him, stretching out his arm, he put his right hand into the flame, which he held so steadfast and unmovable… that all men might see his hand burned before his body was touched. His body did so abide the burning of the flame with such constancy and steadfastness… standing always in one place without moving his body… his eyes were lifted up into heaven.*[11]

The book coloured public opinion of Catholicism as a cruel and oppressive faith.

Left: *A woodcut from John Foxe's* Book of Martyrs. *The first edition had been printed in Latin in 1559 and focused on the persecutions of the Lollards, while the much more complete English edition of 1563 was scathing about Mary's persecutions.*

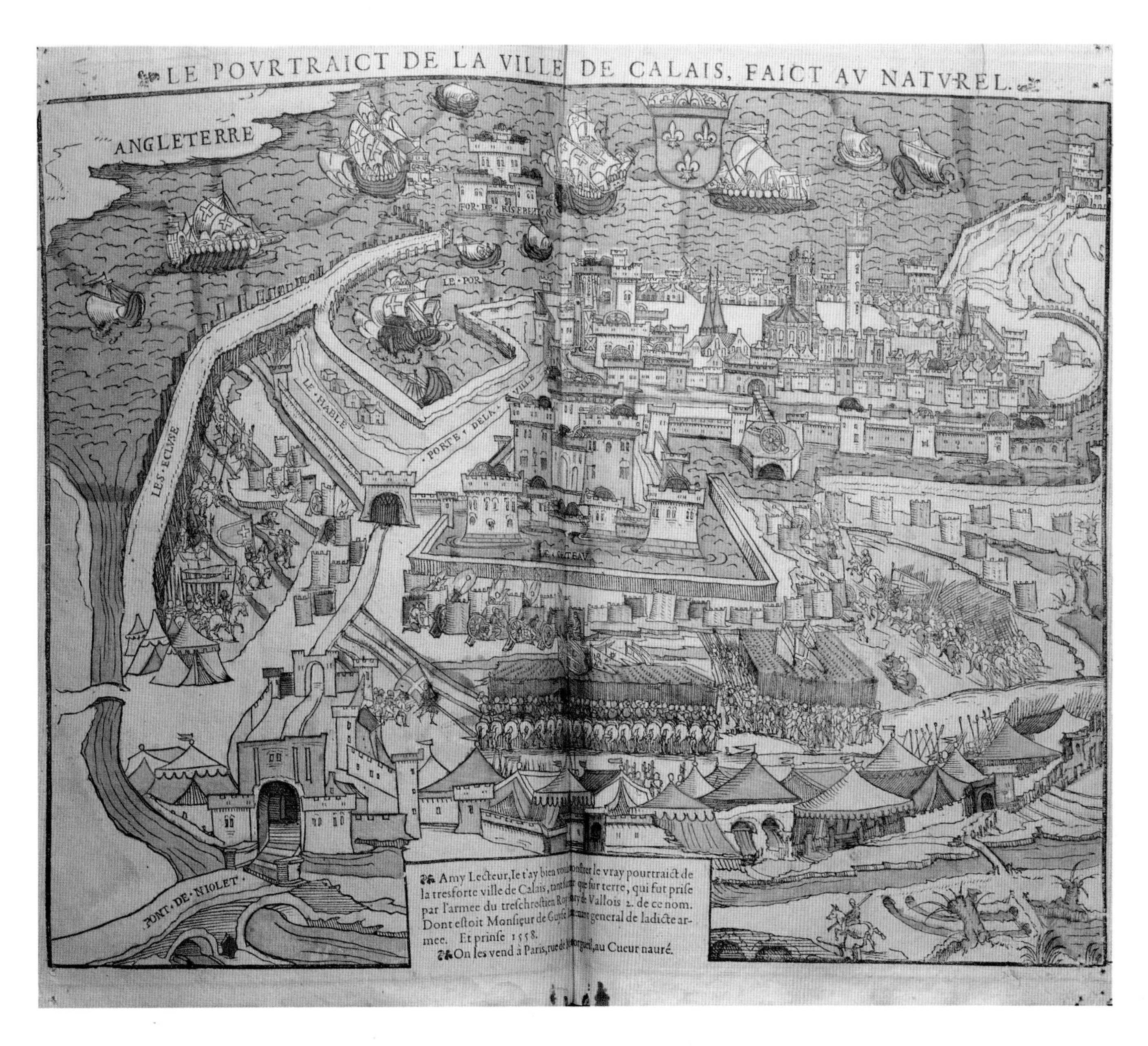

Above: *A contemporary coloured woodcut of the Siege of Calais in 1558. The resistance by the English garrison lasted only six days.*

In any case, the restoration could not succeed in five years; for it to be durable, Mary needed a Catholic successor so she could remove Elizabeth from the succession. She married Philip of Hapsburg, heir to the throne of Catholic Spain, but the couple had no children, and the alliance with Spain dragged England into renewed war with France. Philip became King of Spain in 1556 and the following year persuaded Mary to participate in a campaign in France. England lost Calais, and the English were finally expelled from France in 1558. The conflict frustrated Mary's attempt to restore papal authority; the Pope was allied with France and refused to appoint new bishops in England as Mary wished. That same year, in a further disaster truly out of the monarch's control, a contagion – probably the first flu epidemic – killed around a fifth of the population. Mary herself died in 1558, leaving a country heavily in debt, owing to the cost of the war in France, and divided on religious lines.

ELIZABETH I (1558–1603)

Opposite: *The 'Darnley Portrait' of Elizabeth I,* c. *1575. She took a more tolerant approach to religion than her predecessors.*

Below: *Elizabeth I dancing with Robert Dudley, Earl of Leicester. Dudley was the queen's favourite until he married Lady Essex in 1578.*

In the year that Scottish reformer John Knox declared that the 'imbecility of their sex rendered women unfit to bear rule', Henry VIII's daughter Elizabeth came to the throne and proved otherwise. The reign of this strong and decisive queen saw conflict with Scotland, Ireland and Spain, yet war with France was over, religious tensions were reduced and her rule was mostly harmonious. The reasonably peaceful times were good for trade, and the arts flourished.

THE 'VIRGIN QUEEN'

As a queen ruling without a king, Elizabeth chose her advisers carefully. Early in her reign, she worked with Chief Minister Sir William Cecil (later Lord Burghley) and her favourite courtier Robert Dudley, Earl of Leicester – he courted the queen overtly and it was rumoured she had a relationship with him. Plenty of European royals sought to become her king, too. Elizabeth refused to marry but used her marriage potential as a bargaining chip for playing off France and Spain against each other. Philip II of Spain wanted her for his bride; she refused, but at times when France was a threat, she made it known she might be interested in marrying one of his relatives. Later on, Spain turned against England, so she sought French suitors. Negotiations sometimes continued for months or years but were never concluded.

On the one hand, Elizabeth's strategy appears rational. She had seen how marriage could be a political disaster for women of status. Her mother, Anne Boleyn, had been executed, and her stepmothers had lived and died at the mercy of her father. Most of the foreign princes she could have married were Catholics anyway. Yet she was taking a gamble, for if she died childless, the Tudor dynasty would end. Elizabeth's greatest threat was her cousin Mary, Queen of Scots, the great-niece of Henry VIII, because she had a legitimate claim to the English throne (see below).

MARY, QUEEN OF SCOTS

In 1568, Mary was forced to abdicate the throne of Scotland and fled to England (see page 127). Owing to the threat she presented, Elizabeth kept her cousin prisoner for 19 years. Yet Mary remained the focus of Catholic conspiracies. Parliament often asked Elizabeth to dispose of Mary, but she was unwilling because it made her look cruel. The Babington Plot of 1586 proved to be a turning point. Secretly brought up as a Catholic, Henry Babington was devoted to Mary Stuart and conspired to assassinate Queen Elizabeth and put Mary on the throne, with Spanish assistance. He wrote to Mary outlining his plans, but their correspondence was intercepted and the scheme uncovered. Parliament demanded Mary's arrest.

In this letter from Queen Elizabeth to Mary, Queen of Scots at the start of her trial in October 1586, the queen's frustration with her cousin is apparent:

> *You have in various ways and manners attempted to take my life and to bring my kingdom to destruction by bloodshed. I have never proceeded so harshly against you, but have, on the contrary, protected and maintained you like myself. These treasons will be proved to you and all made manifest. Yet it is my will, that you answer the nobles and peers of the kingdom as if I were myself present.*[12]

Although the evidence of her complicity was not convincingly proven, Mary was found guilty and executed in 1587 at Fotheringay Castle in Northamptonshire.

Left: *Perceived by Elizabeth as a threat, Mary, Queen of Scots was frustrated at her imprisonment in England and focused all her efforts on securing her release.*

RELIGIOUS COMPROMISE

Elizabeth was a moderate Protestant, and her first significant royal action was to reach a settlement on the religious issue. In 1559, the Acts of Supremacy and Uniformity restored royal control over the Church, unifying the state and Church under the monarch. The queen's title became Supreme Governor. Protestant church services were reintroduced, but the system of archbishops and bishops remained. Elizabeth opposed the 'hotter sort of Protestants' – the Puritans who wanted religious reform to go further. Under Elizabeth, there were to be no 'windows into men's souls'. Outward conformity was expected, but people could think what they liked. This compromise allowed the establishment of a secure Church of England.

Despite the firm basis of Protestantism in England, resistance by supporters of a Catholic restoration persisted. In the 1580s and 1590s, various plots were hatched to put Mary, Queen of Scots on the throne, endangering Elizabeth's life. Elizabeth retaliated with anti-Catholic laws that led to the persecution and execution of Catholics in the latter years of her reign.

Favouring unity, the queen supported the Protestant Reformation in Scotland and Ireland to bring them into line with England. A noble faction in Scotland backed the Reformation, winning the struggle for religious reform, and Protestantism was adopted as the country's religion in 1560 (see pages 125–127). In the same year, the Protestant Reformation was introduced by law in Ireland. It was rejected by the majority Catholic population and led to widespread resistance. A major revolt erupted in 1593 under the Earl of Tyrone, which was finally quashed a week after the queen's death. Yet the Irish people would continue to resist the imposition of Protestantism.

A QUEEN'S RESPONSE

In this letter in 1559, Queen Elizabeth responded stridently to an address from five bishops who wished to continue her predecessor's Catholic policies:

> *Our realm and subjects have been long wanderers, walking astray, whilst they were under the tuition of Romish pastors, who advised them to own a wolf for their head (in lieu of a careful shepherd) whose inventions, heresies and schisms be so numerous, that the flock of Christ have fed on poisonous shrubs for want of wholesome pastures.*

She ended her letter with a stark caution:

> *We give you, therefore, warning, that for the future, we hear no more of this kind, lest you provoke us to execute those penalties enacted for the punishing of our resisters...* [13]

Right: *Hugh O'Neill, the second Earl of Tyrone, led a rebellion in Ireland lasting from 1593 until 1601.*

A GOLDEN AGE

The Elizabethan era of stability allowed the arts to flourish. Country houses were built, including Longleat and Hardwick Hall, while musicians, writers and painters sought patronage among the wealthy. The Elizabethan period is known as a Golden Age of literature, when Francis Bacon wrote his celebrated essays and Edmund Spenser his epic poem *The Fairie Queene,* an allegorical work praising Queen Elizabeth. William Shakespeare was an actor and playwright at this time; the queen was his royal patron and watched several of his plays at special court performances. After her death, he eulogized her in Cranmer's speech in the final scene of *Henry VIII:*

She shall be, to the happiness of England,
An aged princess; many days shall see her,
And yet no day without a deed to crown it.
Would I had known no more! but she must die, –
She must, the saints must have her, – yet a virgin;
A most unspotted lily shall she pass
To the ground, and all the world shall mourn her.[14]

Above: *Shakespeare reading to Elizabeth I, from an 19th-century painting.*

Above: *A 16th-century painting of the Spanish Armada of 1588. The Armada consisted of about 130 ships.*

THE SPANISH ARMADA

King Philip II of Spain was also determined to oppose Elizabeth's Protestant nation, and tensions between England and Spain dominated the last years of her reign. In 1588, the Spanish Armada reached the English Channel, aiming to invade England, overthrow Elizabeth and restore the Catholic Church. The English navy roundly defeated the Armada in a battle that became a national legend.

DEFEAT OF THE SPANISH ARMADA

Naval commander Sir Francis Drake announced the English victory against the Armada in a letter to the queen:

> *On fridaye last, upon good consideracion we lefte the army of Spagne so farre to the northewardes, as they could neither recover England nor Scottland. And within three daies after we were entertayned with a great storme, considering the tyme of the yere, the which storme, in many of our judgmentes hath not a litle annoyedd the enemies army. If the wind hinder it not, I think they are forced to Denmark, & that for diverce causes. Certain it is that manie of their people were sick and not a fewe killed, there shippes, sailes ropes & mastes needeth great reparations for that they had all felt of your Majestie's force…* [15]

Few of the Armada's ships survived damage, poor weather and shortages of supplies to return to Spain, and England was saved from invasion.

Opposite: *A portrait of Francis Drake, c.1580.*

Below: *An English fleet under the command of Sir Francis Drake sails into the port of Santo Domingo in the modern Dominican Republic, from a contemporary engraving.*

SENSE OF DUTY

Religion was not the only cause of conflict with Spain. In the relatively stable, peaceful conditions of Elizabeth's reign, English adventurers including Francis Drake and John Hawkins travelled on voyages of discovery to the Caribbean to seek new trading partners. Upon realizing that Spanish ships had already arrived and claimed a monopoly on trade, they shamelessly stole from their Spanish rivals. In 1572, Francis Drake returned from a voyage to the Caribbean with a hoard of Spanish treasure, and in 1577 Elizabeth secretly sent him on a mission to plunder further riches from the Spanish colonies in the Americas. She was thus personally involved in ventures to enrich the realm, providing ships and sharing the profits, and her actions led the way for the expansion of trade and colonization of distant lands. As queen, she perceived it as her duty to increase the power of her realm.

Elizabeth's reign came to a natural end with her death at Richmond Palace on 24 March 1603, apparently after she had named James VI of Scotland as her heir. She had had a significant personal impact, establishing the principle of female authority, cultivating the image of the monarchy and laying the foundations for moderate Protestantism.

CHAPTER 9

RENAISSANCE SCOTLAND 1424–1625

In 15th-century Scotland, the Stewart kings promoted the Renaissance, which led to far-reaching social change and religious revolution. Conflict between the Catholic Church and the Protestant movement swept the country, and the Protestant Reformation triumphed, forcing the Catholic Mary, Queen of Scots to abdicate. After James succeeded to the English Crown in 1603, the monarchy shifted to England, but Scotland retained control of its internal affairs.

SCOTTISH MONARCHS

James I (1424–37)
|
James II (1437–60)
|
James III (1460–88)
|
James IV (1488–1513)
|
James V (1513–42)
|
Mary (1542–67)
|
James VI (1567–1603) and James I of England (1603–25)

Left and below: *Both sides of a coin from the reign of James III, showing the monarch wearing an imperial crown.*

Opposite: *A portrait of James IV. His marriage to Margaret Tudor in 1503 linked the English and Scottish royal houses.*

THE STEWART 'EMPERORS'

The House of Stewart – first established in 1371 by Robert II – claimed a long royal lineage in Europe; the Stewarts saw themselves as emperors with supreme power, like the Holy Roman Emperor. Indeed, James III's coins show him wearing an imperial crown. Yet the family did not have total power: the nobility and senior churchmen controlled the top military and political positions. The nobles often fought among themselves, and they could topple a king if they were displeased with him; James I was assassinated by nobles, and James III died fighting a rebel group. The Stewarts extended their power through marriage. Marrying into European royal families increased their links with Europe and the exchange of ideas that led to the Renaissance.

IACOBVS · 4 · D · GRATIA
REX · SCOTORVM

EDUCATION AND IDEAS

King James I (1424–37) – who was well educated in philosophy, law and theology – and James III (1460–88) are credited with promoting the Renaissance in Scotland, which became fully fledged under James IV and V. James IV was a great patron of the arts and sciences, and in his reign the first printing press was established in Edinburgh. As elsewhere in Europe, the printing press was key to spreading the rediscovered knowledge of the Ancient Greeks and Romans.

Latin was the common language for the proliferation of ideas, and Latin grammar schools and the universities of St Andrews, Glasgow and Aberdeen were founded to promote education. Scottish kings used the power of print to develop national identity; in 1507, James IV gave a licence to the first printers in Scotland to publish patriotic publications in the Scottish language. But the monarchy could not control the realm of beliefs. Ideas that challenged the existing order were also disseminated – in the 1500s, the principles of Protestantism spread like wildfire across Europe.

Below: *King's College at Aberdeen University, which was founded in 1495 by James IV.*

Above: *A portrait of James V and his wife Mary of Guise. During his reign, James consolidated Scottish royal power.*

THE SCOTTISH REFORMATION

The Reformation of 16th-century Europe sparked conflict between Catholicism and the new Protestant movement. In Scotland, the Kirk (Church) was central to Scottish people's lives – it was responsible for education, health and welfare. People believed it was essential to behave in the right way in this world to ensure a happy afterlife with God. Many Scots were interested in the Protestant ideas of a direct relationship between the individual and God, with no bishops or priests as intermediaries. James V tried to ban the Protestant books that appeared, and Scotland remained Catholic – for the time being.

When James V died in 1542, his French-Catholic widow, Mary of Guise, ruled Scotland as regent for her daughter, Mary, Queen of Scots. Scotland was plunged into crisis as France and England tussled for control of the Scottish throne. France was Catholic, while England was newly Protestant, and both countries were desperate to arrange a marriage to the young queen. Henry VIII pushed Mary to marry his son Edward. Diplomacy failed, so in 1544, his troops invaded Scotland; in 1547, much of southern Scotland was occupied by English forces. France helped the Scots to fight back, and they succeeded. England's 'Rough Wooing' policy had failed. Mary of Guise sent her daughter to France for her safety, later arranging for her to marry François, heir to the French crown.

Mary of Guise proved an effective ruler, and it looked as though Scotland would come under French Catholic control. Scotland became allied with France and Mary appointed French officials to powerful positions in Scotland – a Frenchman was appointed head of the treasury, for example. Mary went on a justice ayre (the Scottish

Above: *A stained glass window from St Giles Cathedral, Edinburgh, shows John Knox preaching to an audience.*

form of 'eyre', a circuit court) to settle feuds between the clans.

Meanwhile, pressure on the Catholic Church in Scotland was building. It was unpopular for demanding rents from tenants living on its land and levying taxes, and the Protestant religion was growing rapidly in towns. Scottish nobles saw how their counterparts in England had seized land from the Church under Henry VIII and desired the same opportunity. In 1558, only around 10 per cent of Scots were Protestant. But they now rose up, bringing the militant Protestant John Knox back from exile. He declared there should be no compromise with Catholicism and that it was right to revolt against it: 'In religion there is nae middes (middle): one is either of God, or the Devil'.[1] In May 1559, Knox preached a revolutionary sermon in St John's Kirk in Perth, rousing the congregation to attack the town's monasteries. Queen Mary tried to crush the rebellion, but it spread to Dundee, Scone, Stirling, Linlithgow and Edinburgh. Protestant mobs attacked monasteries and smashed altars, relics and icons in churches to rid them of the trappings of Catholicism. The rebels also claimed they were trying to rid Scotland of French influence.

In England, Queen Elizabeth was also troubled by Scotland's links with France. In 1560, worried that France might take control of her northern neighbour in an effort to deal with the Protestant revolt, she sent a fleet to Firth of Forth to cut off Mary's supply line from France. The threat of war with England led to a peace treaty according to which France would no longer be involved in Scotland, and Scotland adopted Calvinism as the state religion. By 1560, most nobles supported the

THE PERTH REBELLION

John Knox described the masses rampaging in Perth:

> *'In this they were so busy and so laborious that, within two days, these three great places, monuments of idolatry, to wit, the monasteries of the Grey and Black thieves and that of the Charterhouse monks (a building of a wondrous cost and greatness) were so destroyed that only the walls remained.'*

He noted that:

> *'Idolatry was the occasion of the first outburst, but thereafter the common people began to look for spoil.'*

Ordinary people coveted the luxurious possessions of many of the monasteries.[2]

Above: *An illustration of the destruction of the Carthusian Monastery in Perth in 1559.*

CALVINISM

John Calvin (1509–64) was a leading figure in the Protestant Reformation. He agreed with the Protestant critique of the Catholic doctrine of transubstantiation – that the communion bread and wine did not turn into the body and blood of Jesus Christ. For Calvin, although Christ's body was not present, his spirit was everywhere. In church, Calvinists believed that the congregation should sing Psalms but that in general, art and music should play no part in religious devotion; this practice was adopted in Scotland when the country became Protestant. Churches no longer contained images of saints or of Christ on the cross; a plain cross was preferred.

Protestant rebellion. The Scottish Parliament rejected the authority of the Pope, and saying mass became illegal. Scotland had become a Protestant country.

MARY, QUEEN OF SCOTS

After her husband, François II, died unexpectedly in 1561, Mary, Queen of Scots returned to Scotland, the rightful heir to James V's throne. Now that the Protestant Kirk had been established, the Catholic Mary was considered a threat. The following few years proved tense. Mary remarried, to Lord Darnley, but in 1567 he was murdered; she was implicated in the plot but her involvement was never proved. She subsequently married one of the suspected killers, James Hepburn, a man with many enemies. The Scottish nobles decided the queen was a liability; they rose up and imprisoned her in 1567. Six weeks later, Protestant radicals launched another coup d'état and forced Mary to abdicate in favour of her baby son, James VI. Mary escaped to England, where her cousin Elizabeth also incarcerated her. Six years of civil war followed, between the queen's supporters and the Protestant faction. The Protestants gained the upper hand, and by 1573 they had enforced a Protestant regime in Scotland.

Above: *A 16th-century portrait of James VI at eight years old.*

KING JAMES VI

The Protestant Kirk believed it was above the king and should run its own institutions. To James, this was a challenge to royal authority. Although he had only achieved the Crown owing to a rebellion against his mother that had occurred in his infancy, James was nevertheless convinced he was divinely appointed and that he should control the Church. Contrary to the Calvinist view that there should be no bishops as intermediaries in the Church, James insisted on appointing bishops to run the Church. He famously coined the phrase 'No Bishop, no King' and it became his defining motto. In 1618, as king of both England and Scotland, James tried to bring the Kirk in line with the Church of England through the Five Articles of Perth. It included practices of private communion and confirmation by bishops. There was great opposition to the Articles, which were repealed 20 years later. It had become hard for a monarch to impose his will against the wishes of the people.

CHAPTER 10

THE STUARTS 1603–1714

When James VI of Scotland came to the English throne as James I in 1603, a single monarch ruled England and Scotland for the first time. But when he also attempted to govern Ireland, there was widespread resistance. The Stuart dynasty experienced even greater difficulties – two kings were forced off the throne. In 1649, the monarchy faced the biggest crisis in its history: Charles I was executed and Britain became a republic. When the monarchy was restored in 1660, its power was starting to wane. James II and William III both traded the independence of the Crown for assistance in waging war. In 1707, the Act of Union joined England and Scotland to become Great Britain. Britain became a more powerful nation, but the monarchy was permanently weakened.

STUART MONARCHS

James I (1603–25)
|
Charles I (1625–49)
|
Interregnum (1649–60)
|
Charles II (1660–85)
|
James II (1685–88)
|
William III (1689–1702)
and Mary (1689–94)
|
Anne I (1702–14)

Note that the original Scottish name of 'Stewart' is changed to 'Stuart' when referring to the dynasty's rule in England.

JAMES I (1603–25)

James I was no stranger to kingship – he had ruled as James VI of Scotland since infancy (see page 127). A highly educated man, he was a gifted intellectual who wrote persuasively of the role of the monarchy as the divinely appointed mediator between the Church and the state. He aimed to unify England and Scotland under one ruler and one religion, and instigated harsh policies to try to subjugate Ireland too. James accepted that kings were subject to the law but he had frequent disputes with Parliament over money.

James personally took on the complex scholarly project of producing a new English translation of the Bible. Forty-seven scholars in six companies worked on separate sections. They worked hard to imitate the rhythm and style of the original Hebrew, and used the familiar English versions of names, such as Jonah rather than Yonah. Printed in 1611, the King James Bible was a fine literary achievement; it was commonly accepted as the standard English Bible until the early 20th century.

Opposite: *A portrait of James I from 1605. After he became king of England, he returned to Scotland only once more during his lifetime.*

Above: *A contemporary engraving of the leading conspirators involved in the Gunpowder Plot.*

THE GUNPOWDER PLOT

The first major challenge to James's rule came in 1605. A group of Catholics, led by Robert Catesby, were furious that the king had not granted toleration of their faith. They plotted to blow up Parliament and assassinate the king and Members of Parliament (MPs). The plot was discovered after an MP, Lord Monteagle, received an anonymous letter warning him not to attend Parliament on 5 November. He alerted the authorities, and during a search of the Parliament building late on the night of 4 November, Guy Fawkes was discovered in the cellar along with 36 barrels of gunpowder. The following night, Londoners, who knew only that the king had been saved, lit bonfires in celebration. On 31 January 1606, most of the conspirators were hung, drawn and quartered for treason in barbarous executions typical of the time. James had been prepared to be fairly tolerant about religion, but the plot led to anti-Catholic feelings, and the government introduced strict restrictions on Catholics. They were banned from practising law, serving in the army or navy, or voting in elections, amounting to discrimination of the entire community because of the conspiracy of a tiny group.

An extravagant king who lavishly created 1,000 new peers in the first year of his reign, James was forced to bargain with Parliament to replenish his dwindling funds. Some of his requests for grants were authorized, but in return, Parliament insisted on the right to discuss his domestic and foreign policies, and scrutinize his expenditure. James asked them to leave such affairs to the king and his Council and dissolved Parliament in 1611. He called just

GUY FAWKES DAY

In January 1606, Parliament declared that every 5 November would be a day of thanksgiving for the failure of the Gunpowder Plot. In Britain and the American colonies, it became a festival of anti-Catholic sentiments, as crowds gathered to burn effigies of the Pope. In recent decades, Guy Fawkes has been adopted in some circles as a revolutionary hero, with activists donning Guy Fawkes masks for protests against politicians, banks and other financial institutions.

one Parliament between 1611 and 1621 – the so-called Addled Parliament of 1614. It started criticizing government policy, so James dismissed it immediately. A similar situation occurred in 1621, when James called Parliament and requested £500,000. Parliament voted just £150,000. In return, it insisted that England go to war against Spain and impeached Lord Chancellor Francis Bacon for corruption. Since Parliament was interfering in all of his business, James dissolved it.

DRAWN INTO WAR

The last years of James's reign were marked by intensifying pressure for war. His Protestant son-in-law Frederick was chosen by the nobility as King of Bohemia. But the Catholic Holy Roman Empire, ruled by Emperor Ferdinand II and supported by Catholic Spain, was occupying Bohemia and regarded it as its territory. Spanish-led forces attacked Bohemia. James had pro-Spanish leanings and was keen on an English–Spanish alliance, but Parliament and public opinion in general were extremely critical of his approaches to the Catholic nation and put pressure on the king to switch sides. During the last 18 months of his reign, the elderly king was no longer in charge. In 1624, England joined an alliance with Protestant European countries, including Holland and Denmark, with the aim of restoring Frederick to his lands. When James died in 1625, Britain was on the verge of war with Spain. Gradually, all of Europe would be drawn into what became known as the Thirty Years' War.

Although he had battles with Parliament, James had some success in mediating among Protestant groups to end the divisions within the Church of England. Upon accession to the throne, he made peace with Spain after the tensions of the late Elizabethan period. In Ireland, however, it was a different story. Intent on making it part of Britain, James settled thousands of Scottish and English Protestants in the north, giving them land. This created anger and resentment among the local Catholic population and laid the ground for future conflict.

Below: *An illustration showing King James I presiding over Parliament. He prorogued Parliament during its first session of his reign in 1604, setting a pattern that would continue throughout his rule.*

CHARLES I (1625–49)

James's second son, Charles, became heir to the throne when his brother Henry died in 1612. Charles loved the arts, horses and hunting, and was deeply religious, but he was a stubborn man. His reign is a story of confrontation between the powers of the monarchy and Parliament over the right to control government ministers and the country's finances. Charles's failure to compromise cost him his throne and his life, leading to civil war and a halt in monarchical rule.

Opposite: *A portrait of Charles I painted by Anthony van Dyck in 1636. He was a firm believer in the divine right of kings – that his authority came directly from God, rather than the people.*

THE KING vs PARLIAMENT

The tensions between the king and Parliament focused partly on religion. In 1625, Charles married a Roman Catholic, Henrietta Maria of France; in his marriage contract, he secretly added a commitment to remove all barriers to Roman Catholics (see page 130). The marriage was unpopular. Memories of the plots to topple Elizabeth and the Gunpowder Plot against his father were still fresh in people's minds, and Protestants were suspicious that Charles might try to reintroduce Catholicism and renew the religious upheavals of the previous century.

Finance was another major area of contention. Charles believed in his royal prerogative and was determined not to be limited by Parliament. From 1625 to 1629, the king had to choose between securing parliamentary funding and being subject to scrutiny or funding his wars without parliamentary subsidy. He dissolved two Parliaments in 1625 and 1626 because the House of Commons had refused to vote him money unless he accepted that his favoured ministers were responsible to Parliament. Charles became involved in expensive foreign wars on the advice of those favoured ministers, which he financed by taking loans from his subjects without parliamentary consent.

Wars with both France and Spain led to a crisis in 1628–9. There were two failed military expeditions to France, both part of the Thirty Years' War – one was led by Duke of Buckingham, a

Below: *The Duke of Buckingham, in a 1625 portrait by Peter Paul Rubens. He was a favourite of James I and Lord Admiral under Charles I, before his assassination in 1628.*

favourite of Charles. Parliament was greatly angered by the military disasters, and attempted to impeach Buckingham in 1626. To prevent the impeachment, Charles dissolved Parliament. It was clear that the king had the right to choose his ministers, but if Parliament did not like them, confrontation would ensue. The third Parliament of Charles's reign made a complaint about the king's non-parliamentary taxation and imprisonment without trial in the Petition of Right of 1628. Charles signed the petition because he needed money for his wars. He subsequently dissolved Parliament and ruled without it until 1640, making it impossible for Parliament to examine his actions. It was still legal for a king to rule without calling Parliament, but it was an extremely unpopular ploy.

For 11 years, Charles took money directly from his subjects by imposing taxes. One was 'ship money' to pay for a naval fleet. This tax was extended in 1635 from ports to the whole country. The king also obtained funds by exploiting forest laws, imposing forced loans, and taxes on wardships (when a lord became the guardian of a young heir until the individual came of age). These tax burdens caused great rumblings of dissatisfaction.

THE PETITION OF RIGHT, 1628

The petition cited laws made under Edward III (1327–77) declaring that subjects 'have inherited this freedom, that they should not be compelled to contribute to any tax, tallage [arbitrary taxation], aid, or other like charge not set by common consent, in Parliament.'[1] The king was forced to agree to the petition, but the following year, he ordered the dissolution of Parliament. Before it adjourned, Parliament passed three resolutions censuring Charles's behaviour.

ARCHBISHOP LAUD

Earlier suspicions about Charles's Catholic sympathies resurfaced when the king made William Laud the Archbishop of Canterbury in 1633. Laud promoted Laudianism, his own High Church brand of worship which was close to Catholicism. He attempted to restore pre-Reformation practices, such as railing off a communion table to make an altar and bowing to it, which Protestants saw as 'popery'. Such practice was contrary to the Protestant view of the individual's direct relationship with God. Puritans in particular raised their objections. Following riots in Scotland as well as opposition in England, Charles eventually realized that he was exacerbating religious tensions, and in 1640 he changed tack. He abandoned Laudianism, and Laud himself (see The Long Parliament, opposite), and committed to the Protestant faith. He appointed Calvinists to be heads of colleges in Oxford and Cambridge, bolstering Protestant influence.

REBELLION IN SCOTLAND AND IRELAND

In 1637, Charles tried to enforce a High Church liturgy and prayer book in Scotland, designed by the king himself and Archbishop Laud. Riots erupted around the country and the king was forced to call Parliament in April 1640 to request funds to reimpose control. But Parliament refused his entreaties, and Charles dissolved it within five weeks – it became known as the Short Parliament. The Scots took Newcastle and occupied Northumberland and Durham. The following year, the Irish rebelled against Protestant rule in Ireland. Charles was creating enemies all around him.

THE LONG PARLIAMENT

Charles called a further Parliament in November 1640 to seek aid to tackle the Scottish rebellion. This Parliament passed an Act stating that it could not be dissolved without its agreement – it became the Long Parliament. In 1641, Parliament put pressure on the king, ordering that his chief minister, the Earl of Strafford, and Archbishop Laud be imprisoned for high treason for their manipulation of the monarch; they were later executed. In the same year, Parliament passed the Triennial Act, which stated that Parliament had to be called every three years. The king was compelled to agree to it. Parliament also attacked the king directly, in the Grant Remonstrance. It listed his faults and demanded that his ministers be responsible to Parliament. John Pym, the leader of the reform movement in Parliament, now tried to transfer the control of the militia from the Crown to Parliament. The king was incandescent with rage.

In January 1642, Charles stormed into Parliament with an armed guard, hoping to impeach five members of the Commons and one of the Lords for treason. But they had been warned and fled. The Speaker, William Lentall, refused to reveal their whereabouts: 'I have neither eyes to see nor tongue to speak in this place but as this house is pleased to direct me whose servant I am here.'[2] The king replied, 'I see the birds have flown'.[3] His breach of parliamentary privilege – the right to speak freely in the house – lost him the support of many MPs. Pym and his allies once again proposed parliamentary control over the militia and the selection of royal counsellors. Charles refused. In August 1642, he opted to resolve the matter by force. He called on his subjects to support him, and many rallied to the Royalist cause.

Right: *Charles I attempts to arrest five members of the House of Commons for treason in 1642. He was the first English monarch to enter the House of Commons – this was an unprecedented breach of parliamentary privilege.*

Above: *The Battle of Marston Moor, 1644. It was one of the largest military engagements on English soil, involving approximately 40,000 soldiers and causing nearly 5,000 casualties.*

THE ENGLISH CIVIL WAR

England became divided. Charles raised his standard at Nottingham, formally declaring war on 22 August 1642. His Royalists held the North, West and South-West of England, while Parliament's forces, known as the Roundheads, controlled London, East Anglia and the South-East – although there were pockets of resistance in each area. The navy sided with Parliament. Both sides attempted to enlist the Scots as their allies: in 1643, Parliament made an alliance with the Scottish Presbyterian group. From 1644, Parliament began to make gains, achieving victories at the Battles of Marston Moor and Naseby in 1645. In 1646, Charles negotiated with the Scottish Army, hoping it would help him to fight Parliament. As a condition, the Scots asked him to help establish Presbyterianism in England. The king still hoped he might prevail because of divisions among his enemies: faction fighting in Scotland and Ireland, and divisions in Parliament between Presbyterians and Independents. Outside Parliament, the radical Levellers were making demands for social change that threatened the Parliamentary cause. The following year, Charles came to an agreement with the Scots. They would provide him with an army to invade England and he would impose the Presbyterian system on England. He made this agreement, which was against his beliefs, in desperation to regain the throne. But the New Model Army, led by Oliver Cromwell, resisted the Scottish invasion, and in January 1647, the Scots handed Charles over to Parliament. Cromwell was victorious.

OLIVER CROMWELL

Above: *Oliver Cromwell, Lord Protector of England, Scotland and Ireland from 1653 to 1658.*

The only non-royal to rule England, Scotland and Ireland, Oliver Cromwell became a prominent figure in Parliament during the 1640s and rose to become Lord General of the New Model Army. As the conflict with the king escalated, a ferment of political debate arose in the country. Cromwell faced opposition from Members of Parliament, who wanted to replace the Church of England with a Presbyterian Church as in Scotland, and from radicals outside Parliament, who wanted a more democratic form of government, allowing all adult men to vote. Cromwell hoped to reach accommodation with the king so that the monarch would work amicably with him and his allies in Parliament, but when it proved impossible, he led the New Model Army in the civil war against the Royalists, taking power after Charles's execution. Cromwell was also opposed in Ireland and Scotland; in a brutal campaign, his army conquered Ireland in 1649, and in 1650–51 destroyed the monarchist opposition in Scotland, where Charles II had been proclaimed king.

In 1648, the army pressurized the king to abdicate, but he refused. Parliament felt it had no option but to try him for treason against the people; the king declined to plead because he did not recognize the legality of the court. However, the trial began on 20 January 1649 at a specially convened High Court of Justice. Charles was found guilty of treason. On 30 January, he was executed by beheading, outside Whitehall Palace in London. No monarch replaced him; instead, England was ruled as a republic for 11 years, with Oliver Cromwell as head of state. In 1651, monarchists in Scotland crowned Charles's son as King Charles II. The young king marched into England with 10,000 Scottish soldiers, but Cromwell defeated him in the final battle of the civil war, at Worcester. Charles fled into exile in France and did not return to England until he was restored to the throne in 1660.

During the 1650s, Cromwell ruled as a king in all but name. He permitted religious liberty, but arguably he abused his power by imposing taxes without consent and imprisoning his opponents without trial. After Cromwell died in 1658, his government began to fall apart, giving way to the restoration of the monarchy in 1660.[4]

THE LEVELLERS

The Levellers campaigned to improve the lot of working people who endured poverty and deprivation, drawing on Christianity for their ideal of an equal society with no domination by one group over another. As one Leveller explained:

> *'The relation of Master and Servant has no ground in the New Testament; in Christ there is neither bond nor free... The common people have been kept under blindness and ignorance, and have remained servants and slaves to the nobility and gentry.'*[5]

The Levellers called for the sovereignty of the House of Commons, rather than the monarch and lords, and manhood suffrage to elect Parliament.

Above: *John Lilburne, a Leveller, who coined the term 'freeborn rights'.*

CHARLES II (1660–85)

Opposite: *A Restoration-era portrait of Charles II in his garter robes. He returned to England in May 1660 after Parliament welcomed the restoration of the monarchy.*

Below: *The procession of Charles II on the eve of his coronation in 1661. He was the last English monarch to make the traditional journey between the Tower of London and Westminster Abbey before the coronation.*

Charles was forced to live in exile for over a decade, frequently in penury, while believing himself the rightful king of Britain. Embittered by the experience, he was careful, once he achieved his aim of restoration, to make expediency his watchword. He was quick to let ministers take the blame for failed policies rather than sticking by them as Charles I had, and he readily assassinated political opponents. Charles II persecuted Catholics when it suited him although he was secretly a Catholic himself. He managed the power struggle with Parliament far more successfully than his father, but he was ruthless.

Early in his reign, Charles II was relatively conciliatory. He punished those directly responsible for the trial and execution of his father, but pardoned most people who had supported Cromwell's regime. Charles brought his predecessor's enemies into government to get them onside – most of those appointed to the Privy Council and justices of the peace were former Roundheads.

FINANCE THROUGH ALLIANCE

Like his father, Charles hoped to avoid depending on Parliament financially; his strategy was to form alliances in return for money. Between 1667 and 1674, he made secret treaties with the French to fight the Dutch in return for subsidies. In 1674, he made Thomas Osborne the Earl of Danby and his chief minister, with the task of extending the king's influence. Danby switched to a pro-Dutch policy and opposed France; Charles allowed his niece Mary to marry William, the Prince of Orange. Danby persuaded Parliament to fund a war against France, while Charles told Louis XIV that he would abandon his battle plans if Louis paid him – the old medieval strategy (see pages 15–17). Bribery was used to achieve domestic goals too. Danby paid money to the Tory squires to attend Parliament, because they were loyal to the king.

PLAGUE AND FIRE

The double disasters of plague and fire occurred under Charles II's watch. The plague epidemic in 1665 killed about 100,000 people – nearly a fifth of London's population. The Great Fire of London ravaged the city in 1666. Diarist Samuel Pepys witnessed the 'lamentable fire' on 2 September, which was driven through the city's narrow streets and wooden buildings by dry and dusty winds:

> *'Everybody endeavouring to remove their goods, and flinging into the river or bringing them into lighters that layoff; poor people staying in their houses as long as till the very fire touched them, and then running into boats, or clambering from one pair of stairs by the water-side to another.'*[6]

It was the worst fire in the capital's history, destroying 373 acres of the City, from the Tower in the East to Fleet Street and Fetter Lane in the west, burning around 13,200 houses, 84 churches and 44 company halls to the ground.

Above: *A 1675 painting of The Great Fire of London, seen from Tower Wharf.*

WHIGS AND TORIES

During this period, political parties developed in Parliament. The Royalists in the Civil War became the Tories; they accepted the divine right of the monarch to rule and supported the Church of England. They believed the gentry should govern the country under the king and Parliament. The Roundheads became the Whigs. They felt that royal power should be subject to restrictions and that people should have the freedom to worship discreetly as they wished.

Above: *A portrait of James Scott, the Duke of Monmouth.*

CATHOLIC THREAT?

Concerns arose in the 1670s over the succession. Charles had no legitimate children, and his Catholic brother James was heir to the throne. Parliament insisted that James be excluded from the succession, but Charles refused because he was personally committed to Catholicism. However, he responded to alleged Catholic plots with repression. In 1678, rumours circulated that Catholics were planning to murder the king and put James on the throne in a so-called Popish Plot. The rumours were untrue, but they created national hysteria. In a show of strength, the king permitted 35 innocent men to be executed for the non-existent conspiracy.

Charles survived the crisis and re-established control; the final five years of his rule were relatively successful. He converted to Catholicism on his deathbed, and left a Catholic monarch to rule the country. In the contest between the powers of the monarchy and Parliament, perhaps Charles II won this round.

JAMES II (1685–88)

James was crowned James II, King of England and Ireland, but he also reigned as James VII of Scotland. He had converted to Catholicism in 1669 after much soul-searching. Possessing an obstinate nature like his father, Charles I, James was determined to impose Catholicism on the majority Protestant population. Having a Catholic on the throne immediately created conflict. Once more, Parliament and the nobles rebelled, overthrowing this unpopular monarch and inviting a Protestant to replace him.

Within weeks of his accession to the throne, James was faced with rebellions by the Duke of Monmouth in England and the Duke of Argyll in Scotland. In response to this display of distrust by his subjects, James expanded the army and gave command to Roman Catholic officers. He appointed Catholics to high office, made them bishops in the Church of England and replaced nearly half of the justices of the peace with men loyal to him. The king claimed that he was aiming for strict equality between Protestants and Catholics, but since all the institutions of state were Protestant, in effect this meant augmenting Catholic influence. These moves alienated most of the population, including Catholics – they did not trust James and believed he was going too far to reinstate their privileges. In Ireland, where the majority of the people were Catholic, the king suspended all laws against their religious practice. But even here he failed to garner support; he firmly rejected any reversal of the Land Settlement of the 1650s and 1660s which had transferred the ownership of 80 per cent of Irish land to Protestants.[7]

DOWNFALL

In 1687, James dissolved Parliament because it was hostile to him and he never summoned it again. He had also lost the support of most of the nobles by promoting Catholics. When the queen had a son in 1688, Protestant nobles feared he would become a Catholic king – they even claimed he was not her baby and had somehow been smuggled into the palace in a warming pan. This was entirely unjust, yet they used it as an excuse to invite James's Protestant daughter Mary and her husband William of Orange to come from the Netherlands to take the English throne. The army and navy offered their support to William, and James was forced to flee to France. The bloodless Protestant victory became known as the Glorious Revolution, and William and Mary acceded to the monarchy the following year. James mustered the support of French and Irish forces to attempt to regain his Crown, but they were defeated in Ireland at the Battle of the Boyne. The deposed king was forced to spend the rest of his life in exile in France and in Ireland.

Opposite: *A portrait of James II. He believed in the divine right of kings and aimed to restore royal absolutism; his project failed.*

Below: *A lithograph of the landing of William of Orange at Torbay in 1688.*

THE BATTLE OF THE BOYNE

This battle was fought on the banks of the River Boyne some 25 miles (42km) north of Dublin, on 12 July 1690. William III's Protestant army of over 30,000 professional soldiers, armed with the latest flintlock muskets, defeated James's Catholic army, which consisted of poorly equipped Irish peasants backed up by 6,000 French troops. In an eyewitness account, Catholic Jacobite Captain John Stevens claimed that 1,000 Irish Catholic troops drank so extravagantly that they were 'dead drunk scattered about the fields' at the start of the battle. His account also blamed Jacobite commanders for being cowards who fled the field. Was he making excuses for the Jacobite defeat?[8] Whatever the truth of the matter, it was a significant turning point in royal history. To this day, Protestants in Northern Ireland celebrate the battle every year as a victory for the Protestant cause.

Above: *The Battle of the Boyne in 1690. After this battle, James II fled to France and ensured William III's position.*

WILLIAM III (1689–1702) AND MARY II (1689–94)

William and Mary ruled on the invitation of Parliament and could claim no divine right. They had to accept a Declaration of Rights before they were given the Crown, which represented an important shift in political power. The monarchy remained important, but Parliament increased its powers significantly. In religious matters, William and Mary tolerated Protestant dissenters but not Catholics; they were determined to quash any hopes of a Catholic restoration raised under James II. The monarchs ruled jointly although William had all the power – Mary's value lay purely in being a Protestant Stuart and a bulwark against a potential Catholic monarch. William was chiefly concerned with the Netherlands; the English Crown merely provided useful resources for his ongoing struggle against France.

A PROTESTANT MONARCHY

The Bill of Rights excluded Catholics and people married to a Catholic from the monarchy: 'it hath been found by experience that it is inconsistent with the safety and welfare of this Protestant kingdom to be governed by a popish prince'.[9] Every monarch had to swear loyalty to the Protestant faith. In the same year, the Toleration Act gave freedom of religion to all Nonconformists, but not to Catholics. The Act of Settlement of 1701 stated that all future monarchs had to be members of the Church of England.

THE DECLARATION OF RIGHTS

The 1689 Declaration of Rights (later the Bill of Rights) was drawn up by Parliament to limit the power of the monarchy and prevent its abuse. Parliament controlled who could take the Crown and stated that he or she had to be a Protestant. To rule effectively, the monarch had to select ministers who could achieve a majority of votes in the House of Commons and Lords to pass laws. The king could not interfere with proceedings in Parliament, suspend laws that Parliament had passed or administer justice separately from Parliament; he was forbidden to set up his own courts or act as a judge. This was the foundation of parliamentary privilege, which still exists today.

The Declaration also confirmed Parliament's right to control taxation. The king could not raise taxes without permission from Parliament. Every year, the monarch had to ask Parliament to renew funding for the army and navy, and he was not permitted to have his own standing army in peacetime. Thus the Crown was dependent on Parliament for finances, and Parliament had tight control over its expenditure. As one MP said: 'when princes have not needed money, they have not needed us'.[10] The Triennial Act of 1694 re-established the rule, not enforced since 1664, that Parliament had to be elected at least every three years.

The rights of the monarch were clearly defined. He still called Parliament and dissolved it; he could select and dismiss ministers and veto legislation. The monarch had the right to financial support from Parliament; in 1697 Parliament gave the monarch an annual grant of £700,000 for life as a contribution to the expenses of government, which included salaries for ambassadors and judges and the costs of the Royal Household.

Below: *Parliament offers the crown and the Declaration of Rights to William of Orange and Mary Stuart in this 20th-century illustration.*

NATIONAL DEBT

William wished to utilize the English throne as a power base from which to contain French expansion, and to this end, England and the Netherlands fought France from 1689 to 1697. To finance the long and costly Nine Years' War, Parliament set up the National Debt and the Bank of England in 1694, which transformed its role. It now had to be called every year to raise money to pay off the National Debt. This system also meant that the king was reliant on Parliament to finance war; although he could declare war, he could not initiate it without parliamentary consent. William had not intended to make these fundamental changes to the way Britain was governed – he simply wanted money for his wars against France. Yet the changes proved lasting.

THE CABINET

In 1696, William appointed a ministry drawn from the Whigs, called the Junto. It met separately from the Parliament, which at first aroused the suspicion of MPs. This was an early form of the Cabinet and a vital part of the development of the political system – a committee of ministers to manage Parliament. As parliamentary sessions became longer, political parties evolved, and the two-party system of Tory and Whig was solidified. It would last 200 years.

Above: *The Whig Junto in a 1710 painting. The group met in country houses between parliamentary sessions to discuss party policy and strategy.*

ANNE 1702–14

The second daughter of James II and the last monarch to truly believe in her divine right to rule, Anne had a difficult reign. Racked by chronic ill health, she became pregnant 18 times; only three children were born alive, and they all died in their youth. With no Stuart child to succeed her, frictions arose when it became clear Anne would leave no heir. Although her father had been Catholic, she had been brought up as a Protestant, but at this time, the English and Scottish Parliaments decided union might be the best option: England was worried that the Jacobites might try to seize control through Scotland, and Scotland needed economic aid. To seal the bargain, Scotland would accept a Hanoverian Protestant monarch in return for freedom of trade with England. In 1706, the two Parliaments agreed the Treaty of Union between England and Scotland. Under the Act of Union of 1707, they would form a Union Parliament in Westminster. Yet Scotland would maintain internal control, keeping the Kirk and its legal and educational systems.

Opposite: *A portrait of Queen Anne. During her reign, she tried to manage the fierce party rivalry between Whigs and Tories.*

CHAPTER 11

THE HOUSE OF HANOVER 1714–1901

The Act of Settlement of 1701 defined clear rules for the succession to the throne, dictating that the monarch had to be Protestant – but not necessarily British. To prevent James II's Catholic son from becoming king, the title was instead offered to George, whose grandmother Elizabeth was the daughter of James I. George leapt to first in line for the succession ahead of 57 Catholics more closely related to Anne.[1] The House of Hanover retained the succession for several monarchs, despite the challenge of the Jacobites, supporters of the Catholic descendants of James II, who rose up a number of times in favour of the exiled Stuarts. Under the Hanoverians, the monarchy was further restricted in its authority: Parliament could force a monarch to dismiss unpopular ministers. Yet constitutional monarchy was a flexible institution, able to adjust to the character and interests of individual kings and queens. Monarchs could leave the workings of government to politicians, but if they were keen to participate, they could exert some influence.

GEORGE I (1714–27)

Already 54 when he came to the throne, George I knew little about Britain and spoke so little English that his coronation service had to be conducted in Latin. He never learnt to speak English fluently and remained engrossed in ruling Hanover, where he spent a considerable amount of his time. Never a popular monarch, George showed enough political sense to accept the limitations imposed on the monarchy following the 1688 Glorious Revolution and was prepared to adapt to survive.

George distrusted and disliked the Tories, many of whom were sympathetic to the Jacobites. He depended on the Whigs (see page 141), who decisively won the general election in 1715. Acting in a partisan fashion, George dismissed Tories from the armed forces and promoted Whig clerics. By the time the Hanoverian dynasty ended, it would no longer be possible for a monarch to do this.

Contrary to long-established views that he was uninterested in politics, George did attend Cabinet meetings, communicating

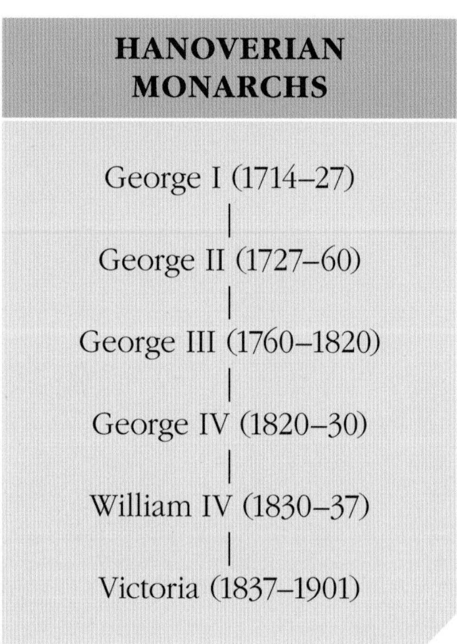

Opposite: *A portrait of George I in his coronation robes from 1714. He was active in foreign policy during the early years of his reign, working closely with the Whigs.*

THE JACOBITE CHALLENGE

The son of James II, the Catholic James Edward Stuart challenged George's claim to the throne. He had support in France, where he lived, and in Spain and in Scotland, and the clans rose up in his favour in 1715. James Stuart arrived in Scotland in December that year, but the insurgency failed. Further Jacobite plots in 1719 and 1722 were also defeated. In 1791, the poet Robert Burns wrote a song about James Stuart, lamenting the loss of the true king of Scotland. The final verse is:

Now life is a burden that bows me down,
Sin I tint [as I lost] my bairns [children], and he tint his crown;
But till my last moments my words are the same –
There'll never be peace till Jamie comes hame [home].[2]

Left: *James Edward Stuart sought to realize his claim to the thrones of England and Scotland in the Jacobite rising of 1715.*

with his ministers in French. He got on well with some of them, particularly James Stanhope and Charles Sunderland. However, Stanhope died in 1721, and Sunderland was held responsible for involving the king in the South Sea Company, which proved disastrous.

THE SOUTH SEA BUBBLE

The South Sea Company was a trading and finance business with heavy government and royal investments; it had expanded so greatly that it hoped to take over the National Debt of £31 million in exchange for company shares. In a fever of speculation, the share price soared. But the bubble burst in 1720, panic selling ensued, and the company was brought to the brink of collapse, leading to a crisis of confidence in the economy. Following Sunderland's death in 1722, the king was forced to rely on Sunderland's Whig rival Robert Walpole to get him out of the mess. Parliament took out its anger on the company rather than the king, confiscating its property and imprisoning some of those responsible for the catastrophe in the Tower of London. Walpole organized this impressive face-saving exercise to avoid

the risk of encouraging the Jacobites. Afterwards, although he hated him, George had to accept Walpole as his chief minister, and Walpole brought stability to the final years of the king's reign.

Above: *An illustration in the style of William Hogarth (1697–1764) depicting the economic crisis following the collapse of the South Sea Company in 1720.*

George II (1727–60)

George II was passionate about military matters and loved to tell stories of his bravery fighting the French in 1708: as head of the Hanoverian cavalry, he had charged the enemy, and his horse was shot from beneath him. The king put pressure on the government to fund the armed forces to extend British power through war. The major challenge of George's reign, just as his father's had been, was the Jacobite threat; many Tories supported James Stuart's son Charles Edward, either openly or secretly. During this period, England became involved in global power struggles over colonies. The king was not particularly enthusiastic about trade or colonies, yet the importance of merchants' economic activities and their ability to shape politics was growing, regardless of the monarchy.

The king still had the power to appoint his own ministers. At times, though, Parliament flexed its muscles, forcing him to dismiss ministers with whom it did not agree. In 1742, after Walpole's fall, George appointed John Carteret – an opponent of Walpole – as Secretary of State. Carteret forcefully prosecuted the War of the

BONNIE PRINCE CHARLIE

In 1745, Charles Edward, the son of James Edward Stuart, presented a serious threat to the monarchy. Known as 'Bonnie Prince Charlie', he travelled from Paris to Scotland to lead a Jacobite uprising in England. George's son William headed the forces that crushed the rebellion at the brutal and bloody Battle of Culloden, near Inverness, in 1746. It was the last time a Stuart attempted to retake the British throne, as the Hanoverian dynasty prevailed after a final harrowing battle..

A Scottish rebel gave an eyewitness account of the Battle of Culloden, in which 1,500 soldiers were slaughtered in less than an hour: 'I saw… Big Iain Gillies cutting down the English as if he was cutting corn and… Freckled Iain Chisholm killing them as though they were flies. But the English were numerous and we were few and a large number of our friends fell. The dead lay on all sides and the cries of pain of the wounded rang in our ears.'[3]

Above: *A 1730 portrait of the young Bonnie Prince Charlie, who escaped Scotland after the defeat at Culloden.*

Left: The Battle of Culloden *by David Morier (1746). The ensuing clampdown to prevent further rebellion earned English army commander, the Duke of Cumberland, the label 'Butcher'.*

Austrian Succession (which had broken out in 1740) in favour of the Austrian princess Maria Theresa. George himself fought at the Battle of Dettingen in 1743, the last time a British monarch engaged in battle. The war was unpopular – Carteret was seen to be prioritizing the king's Hanoverian possessions over British interests – and in 1744, Parliament obliged the king to dismiss him.

Left: *George II at the Battle of Dettingen in 1743.*

Below: *The London Customs House, seen from the River Thames. During the reign of George II, Britain's global footprint greatly expanded, and London became one of the world's most important trading centres.*

INDUSTRIAL REVOLUTION AND COLONIZATION

The foundations of the Industrial Revolution were laid during George II's reign. Agricultural production was booming, accompanied by a rapid rise in the population, and the coal and shipbuilding industries were expanding significantly. Britain was fighting to control territory and dominate trade in Europe, the Caribbean, the Americas, India and Africa. During the Seven Years' War (1756–63), Britain seized French Canada and reduced French influence in India; by the end of the conflict, it was the world's dominant colonial and naval power. Meanwhile, the East India Company, formed in 1600 to develop trade in South-East Asia and India, had also become an agent for British colonization; Robert Clive took administrative control of Bengal in 1757. Such conquests laid the foundations of the British Empire. Although not directly related to George II's rule, the expansion of British prosperity helped to improve his image and he became more popular as his reign continued.

GEORGE III (1760–1820)

Opposite: *A portrait of George III, c. 1775. He was the first Hanoverian king who was born and educated in Britain.*

George III is infamous for his mental illness and often remembered as the king who lost the American colonies, but the true story is more complex than that. Historians continue to debate the reason for his mental decline and it may be unfair to blame him for America's separation from Britain. In many ways, he was a successful king and remains the longest-serving male English monarch. Although less involved than his father in the daily running of government, he retained some political leverage and was respected by many Members of Parliament.

Below right: *A lithograph showing George Washington's triumphal entry into New York City on 25 November 1783.*

THE LOSS OF AMERICA

In the 1760s and 1770s, the British government needed money. It had incurred huge costs during the Seven Years' War (see page 153) and needed to pay for administering the territory it controlled in North America and for new wars with France and Spain to conquer further territory. The government had also lent money to the East India Company for its colonial ventures. In the 1770s, the government required £4 million in interest payments every year to service the national debt.

England saw the American colonies as a handy source of tax revenue, and King George supported Parliament's efforts to extract it. The Stamp Act of 1765 required that all legal documents and other printed materials produced in the

FROM ENEMIES TO FRIENDS?

The king accepted the loss of the American colonies and hoped that America and Britain would develop a friendly relationship. In an essay written some time after the conflict, he wrote:

> *America is lost! Must we fall beneath the blow? Or have we resources that may repair the mischief? ... it is to be hoped we shall reap more advantages from their trade as friends than ever we could derive from them as Colonies.*[4]

After the war, Britain did indeed derive benefits. To help pay off the debts incurred from fighting the war with its former colony, it raised tariffs on American goods and flooded the US market with cheap manufactured goods with which local producers could not compete.

colonies had to be on paper bearing an embossed tax stamp. Americans had to pay the tax in British currency to specially commissioned distributors to acquire the stamped paper. The law applied to wills, deeds, newspapers, pamphlets and even playing cards and dice. The American colonists were furious: they deemed it unfair that they were taxed although they had no representation in the British Parliament. They refused to buy the stamps. George was reluctant to withdraw the tax, but Parliament repealed it in 1766, fearing revolt.

Left: *A one-penny stamp brought in by the Stamp Act of 1765.*

Yet Britain continued to raise revenue by imposing duties on goods imported into the British colonies and tried to exert greater control over American affairs. Resistance to British control developed into a full-scale rebellion in 1775: the American War of Independence. In 1783, following a bitter war, the American colonies defeated Britain and became an independent nation. The king was associated with this disaster for Britain. But some contend that he did not have much responsibility for the defeat; although he opposed the independence of the colonies, it was Parliament that developed the policies which led to war.

Below: *In this satirical print, George III is shown as the King of Brobdingnag and Napoleon as Gulliver, characters from Jonathan Swift's novel* Gulliver's Travels.

THE KING'S PREROGATIVE

The king struggled to deal with the Whig and Tory groups in Parliament and form ministries that could rule effectively, but he found good leaders in Lord North and Pitt the Younger, who both had long, stable ministries – from 1770 to 1772 and 1783 to 1801 respectively. On occasion, he asserted his will. Pitt the Younger dominated politics for two decades, yet when he proposed to grant full civil rights to Catholics, the king withdrew his support. He argued that it went against his coronation oath to protect the Church of England, a move that forced Pitt to resign in 1801.

GROWING POPULARITY

Although he sometimes exerted his authority, the king became less occupied with the day-to-day running of government. He was increasingly seen as above the factional politics of Parliament, which increased his popularity as a national figurehead. George projected

Above: *A portrait of William Pitt the Younger, who became the youngest Prime Minister of Britain when he entered office in December 1783 at the age of 24.*

a sense of domesticity with his family; he was perhaps the first monarch to focus on this aspect of royal life. Furthermore, after the French Revolution of 1789, when France became a republic, the monarchy became a symbol of British identity and continuity in troubled times. It was a way to differentiate Britain from France, still perceived as an enemy nation.

It had been rare for a monarch to remain 50 years on the throne, and George's jubilee was celebrated with gusto around the country. The wealthy enjoyed lavish balls, churches hosted thanksgiving services, and landlords provided feasts of roasted oxen and sheep for the poor. At Lord Bolton's seat in Hackwood, Basingstoke, 'not less than one thousand persons… were liberally treated with an amplitude of wholesome viands, accompanied with ten hogsheads of strong beer.' In London, the façade of the Bank of England was candlelit with illuminations, spelling God Save the King, a spectacular sight.'[5]

THE REGENCY AND WATERLOO

The following year, the king became seriously ill, and agreed to the terms of the Regency Bill in 1811, which deemed him unfit to serve. He passed the reins of power to his son, the Prince of Wales, who acted as regent until his father died in 1820. Though the Prince played little part in the politics of the time, it was a momentous era of social, political and economic change. There was conflict too, as the Napoleonic Wars continued. At the start of the 1800s, Napoleon had become Emperor of France and vowed to achieve mastery of all of Europe. For a few years, his ambitions succeeded. At its height,

THE MADNESS OF KING GEORGE III

Alan Bennett's play, written in 1991, helped popularize the theory that George's illness was caused by a blood disorder called porphyria, which caused pain, blindness and blue urine. Yet research in the 2010s indicates that the king's urine turned blue because he took medicine with the blue-flowered herb gentian, and that he did, in fact, suffer from mental illness. It is likely that he was bipolar; when he was in his 'high' phase, he talked non-stop using colourful language and 400-word sentences, until foam came out of his mouth. When he was depressed, he withdrew to Kew Palace in Richmond to recuperate. George usually recovered and returned to business, but in 1811, his mental capacity declined so drastically that his son adopted the role of regent.

the Napoleonic empire included France, Belgium, Holland, parts of Italy, Croatia and Dalmatia. Standing in his way of full control of the continent was England with its powerful navy, and Horatio Nelson had annihilated the French fleet at the Battle of Trafalgar in 1805.

Napoleon then looked eastwards, hoping to conquer the vast territory of Russia. But his 1812 invasion was a disastrous failure; his troops were defeated by the bitter Russian winter as much as by its army. The nations of Europe seized the moment to rise up against Napoleon, and in 1815 he was finally overwhelmed at the Battle of Waterloo by an Allied force of British, Prussian, Belgian and Dutch soldiers. Napoleon was forced to abdicate and he was exiled from France.

Above: *The Battle of Waterloo, 1815. At Waterloo, the British Duke of Wellington and the Prussian Field Marshal Blücher combined forces to finally defeat Napoleon.*

George IV (1820–30)

George IV's heart lay in art and architecture – he assembled a collection of major works of art and built the extravagant Royal Pavilion in Brighton. Following an elaborate coronation, the new king was well received on visits to Ireland, Hanover and Scotland. But he lacked his father's dedication to royal duties; after 1823, he retreated from public view in London, except for the opening and proroguing (closing) of Parliament.

Fortunately for George, Lord Liverpool's Tory administration was stable from 1812 to 1827. When Lord Liverpool fell ill, it caused a political crisis. Who would succeed him? The king was not particularly concerned about using his royal prerogative; he even suggested that ministers should choose the successor. From 1828, the Tory Lord Wellington became prime minister. At this time, there was pressure to change the law restricting the rights of Catholics, an issue that divided Conservatives. George disagreed with repealing the law, but Wellington forced him to accept the 1829 Catholic Emancipation Act, which allowed Catholics to become MPs. His father had stopped a similar law from passing, but this time the king was unable to override Parliament's decision.

Below: *The coronation of George IV in July 1821. He enjoyed an indulgent lifestyle with much drinking and socializing.*

WILLIAM IV (1830–37)

Above: *An engraving of William IV from 1830.*

Opposite: *A portrait of George IV painted in 1816, while he was still Prince Regent. During the Regency, he left matters of government to the ministers.*

From age 13, William enjoyed an active career in the navy; he later lived with his actress girlfriend Dorothea Jordan, and they had ten children. As the third son of George III, he never expected to become king, but both of his older brothers died and he was propelled to the throne. William's reign was dominated by efforts to pass the Reform Bill, and the king was exhorted to act in line with the desires of the government. From this time onwards, political changes were introduced with the passive as much as active support of the monarch.

THE REFORM BILL

Shortly after William's accession, a Whig government under Lord Grey replaced the Tories. Lord Grey was determined to make the government more representative of the increasingly urban population by extending the franchise to property owners. Large towns such as Manchester and Birmingham still had no MPs, although many 'rotten boroughs' existed – depopulated areas where the Crown or aristocrats controlled seats in the House of Commons. In 'pocket boroughs', the leading landowner bribed the tiny population to elect his representative to Parliament.

In April 1831, the House of Commons rejected Grey's Reform Bill. In a fresh general election, Grey won again, and made a second attempt to pass the bill. The Lords rejected it, and rioting in favour of reform erupted around the country. In June 1832, Grey asked the king to create 50 new Lords to overcome Tory opposition to the bill in the Commons and Lords. William refused, and Grey threatened to resign. The king caved in and agreed to create enough new peers to pass the bill. He had been persuaded that there would be widespread disorder if he refused, and was encouraged to support reform.

The Reform Act finally passed in 1832. It altered the political balance between the Crown, the Commons and the Lords. With new boroughs and a wider electoral franchise, the Commons gained at the expense of the Lords. The abolition of rotten and pocket boroughs meant that powerful landowners could no longer control access to the Commons. The Crown was unable to interfere directly in parliamentary politics because it did not have its own MPs in the Commons; the monarch had to exercise power indirectly through negotiation with people in power. William did use his prerogative in 1834 to dismiss Melbourne's Whig government, but his attempts at power-broking failed. The following year, the Tories lost the election, and Melbourne was returned to power anyway.

REFORMING ROYALS

William was seen publicly to be supporting political reform and acting as a constitutional monarch. He once said, 'I have my view of things, and I tell them to my ministers. If they do not adopt them, I cannot help it. I have done my duty.'[6] There was a sense that the monarchy was on the side of progress, which greatly benefited the institution.

Above: *A painting by William Hogarth illustrating the corruption of 18th-century elections. The 1832 Reform Act made for a fairer system, but the electorate saw only a relatively small increase, from 400,000 to 650,000.*

VICTORIA (1837–1901)

'I shall do my utmost to fulfil my duty towards my country; I am very young… but I am sure, that very few have more real good will and more real desire to do what is fit and right than I have.'[7] Eighteen-year-old Victoria wrote these words on the day that she came to the throne. During her regency, the monarchy continued to evolve; she had less power than her predecessors and the institution became more symbolic, focusing on grand ceremonies and royal rituals. However, Victoria's status was boosted by being associated with the British state at a time of great national wealth and power, achieved through industrial growth, economic progress and a burgeoning empire that reached its peak towards the latter part of her 63-year reign.

Opposite: *A portrait of Victoria as princess in 1833. As the heir to the throne, she made regular tours around the country.*

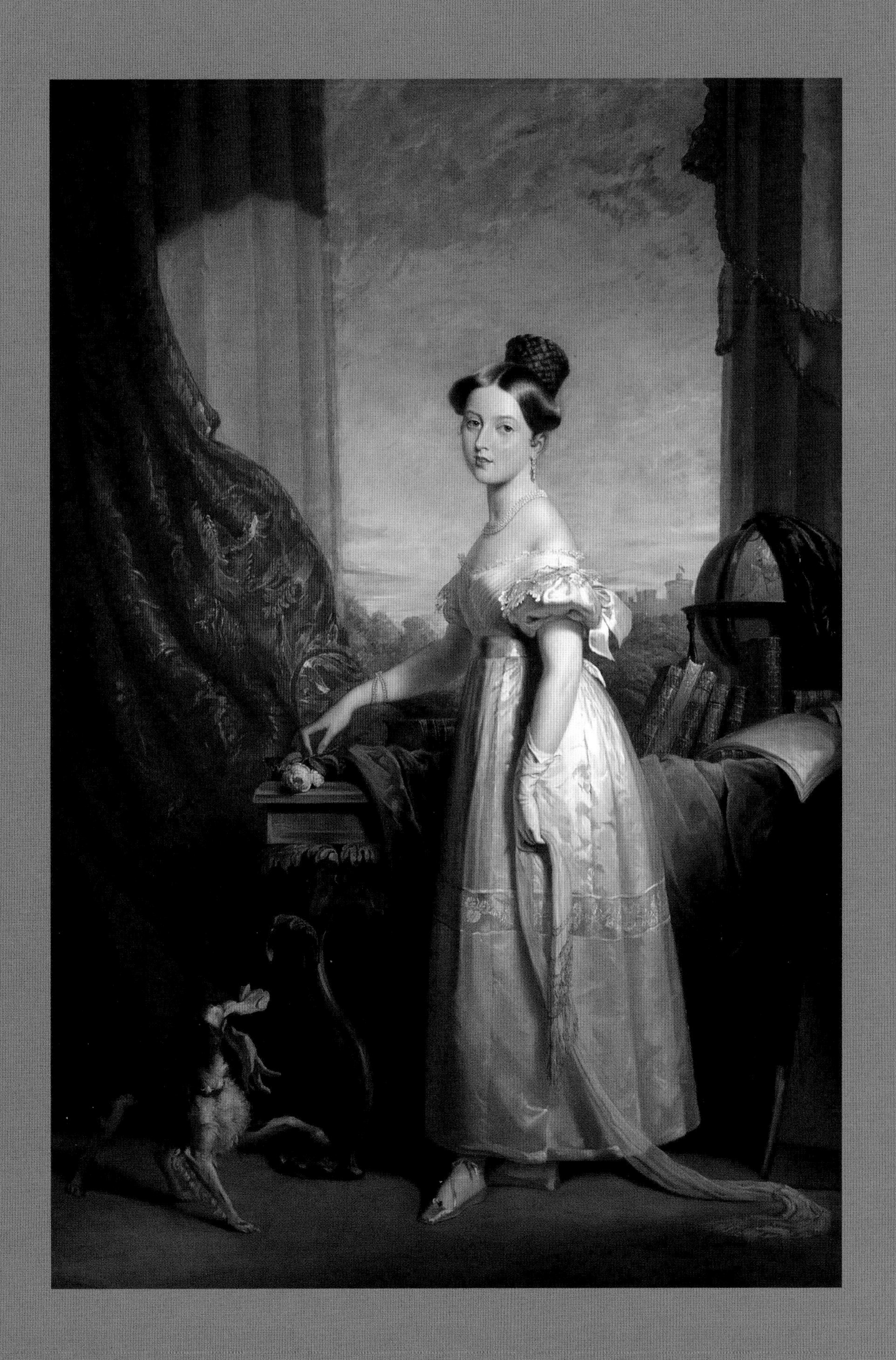

PARTISAN POLITICS

Early in her reign, Queen Victoria openly identified with Whig Prime Minister Lord Melbourne. In 1839, the Whig government fell, and Lord Melbourne resigned. Tory leader Robert Peel agreed to become prime minister if the queen replaced some Whig Ladies-in-waiting with Tory ones, so that their political allegiances would be more neutral, but she refused. As a result, Peel refused to accept the post. To prevent a constitutional crisis, Lord Melbourne and the Whigs agreed to serve again. After Victoria's marriage to Prince Albert, Melbourne, who praised his 'judgement, temper and discretion', was keen for the prince to be involved in government. Victoria gave birth to nine children between 1840 and 1857, during which time Albert's political role increased. In 1845, clerk of the Privy Council Charles Greville stated that 'while she has the title, he is really discharging the functions of the Sovereign. He is the King to all intents and purposes.'[8] In contrast to Victoria, Prince Albert believed that a constitutional monarch should remain aloof from party politics and be politically impartial.

CEREMONIAL ROLES

Although she began to defer political responsibilities to her husband, Queen Victoria developed an interest in social welfare issues, such as child labour, and participated in novel ceremonies and duties that would help to ensure the survival of the monarchy.

Above: *Lord Melbourne was Prime Minister between 1834 and 1841, apart from a few months after he was dismissed by William IV.*

Left: *Queen Victoria with her family, painted in 1846.*

Opposite: *An engraving of the wedding of Queen Victoria and Prince Albert in 1840.*

In 1852, she attended the first State Opening of Parliament in the new Palace of Westminster, arriving in an ornate Irish State Coach. She processed through Parliament and made a speech. All monarchs have continued this custom ever since. Victoria and her family visited provincial towns to open buildings and attend important dinners. Improvements in transport facilitated their travel around the country – Victoria was the first monarch to use a train in 1842. Ordinary people were able to view Victoria and her family more easily than previous monarchs. With the spread of newspapers and photography, people across the nation could read stories and see photographs of royal family life, and their births, marriages and funerals became public events.

Above: *A 19th-century painting of the Charge of the Light Brigade, a disastrous military engagement for the British during the Crimean War.*

With a reduced political role, the royal family was obliged to demonstrate its worth to the nation. Victoria became the patron of 150 institutions, including many charities. Albert associated himself with science, trade and industry, all of which were developing at a phenomenal rate. He promoted the Great Exhibition of 1851, the first international exhibition of industrial products, and contributed to its huge success. The prince also supported educational museums; the profits from the Great Exhibition were used to establish the Natural History Museum, the Science Museum and the Victoria and Albert Museum in London. The aim was to showcase British achievements – the South Kensington area was affectionately nicknamed 'Albertopolis'.

RISING REPUBLICANISM

Following the death of her beloved Albert in 1861, from what was described as typhoid, Victoria withdrew from public life. The queen was devastated; she declined to attend Albert's funeral, ordered the court to enter a period of two years of mourning and took to wearing only black clothes. She dealt with official correspondence and met ministers and official visitors but refused to appear in public. Victoria was publicly criticized for her hermit-like behaviour. In addition, the founding of the French Third Republic in 1870 led to a rise in republican feelings in Britain. It was vital for the monarch to return to the forefront of British affairs. The queen re-emerged in 1871, sharing her concerns about her son Edward, who had fallen ill with typhoid. Fortunately, he recovered, and she held a public thanksgiving service, using his recuperation to mark her return to public life and boost support for the monarchy.

Below: *A photograph of Benjamin Disraeli taken in 1878.*

SYMBOLIC STATUS

The status of the monarchy also revived with the expansion of the British Empire. Conservative Benjamin Disraeli (prime minister 1868, 1874–80) was a keen supporter of British imperialism, and Victoria heartily approved. In 1877, on Disraeli's advice, Victoria adopted the title Empress of India. The title increased her status further; in the public mind, she had become a symbol of British dominance in the world.

THE OPENING OF THE GREAT EXHIBITION, 1 MAY 1851

Victoria described what she saw on her arrival at the Hyde Park site:

> *'The sight… facing the beautiful crystal fountain was magic and impressive. The tremendous cheering, the joy expressed in every face, the vastness of the building, with all its decorations and exhibits… and my beloved Husband the creator of this great "Peace Festival", uniting the industry and arts of all nations of the earth.'*[9]

Left: *The Crystal Palace in Hyde Park, the location of the Great Exhibition of 1851.*

Left: *The Royal Procession during the Golden Jubilee of 1887. The procession was preceded by a lavish banquet attended by 50 kings, princes and overseas governors.*

Opposite: *A lithograph of Queen Victoria in 1887, created at the time of her Golden Jubilee.*

Victoria's popularity revived towards the end of her reign. Impressive shows of pomp and ceremony were organized for her Golden Jubilee in 1887 and Diamond Jubilee ten years later. In *The English Constitution*, Walter Bagehot had described the mystique of monarchy: the idea that although the monarchy had less political power, it had a greater symbolic role. He was remarkably prescient, for this turned out to be the future of the monarchy.[10]

THE BRITISH EMPIRE

By the time Victoria came to the throne, Britain had colonized Australia, New Zealand, Canada, much of India, Ceylon (now Sri Lanka), parts of Burma (now Myanmar), parts of the Caribbean and other areas. Following the Indian Mutiny of 1857, the British government took over direct rule of India. The greatest area of growth of the empire in the 19th century was in Africa. From 1880, Britain occupied or annexed a vast swathe of countries right across the continent, including Egypt in the north to Kenya in the east, Ghana in the West and Zimbabwe in the south. As its height, the British empire covered over 14 million square miles of territory in which over 450 million people lived – more than a quarter of the world's population. Thus British commercial, political and economic dominance spread across the globe.

THE GRANDMOTHER OF EUROPE

Queen Victoria and Prince Albert had nine children, many of whom married into other royal families across the Continent, and Victoria is often known as the Grandmother of Europe since so many of her descendants eventually ruled in countries as far afield as Russia and Spain.

The family tree below shows Queen Victoria's children and their most prominent offspring.

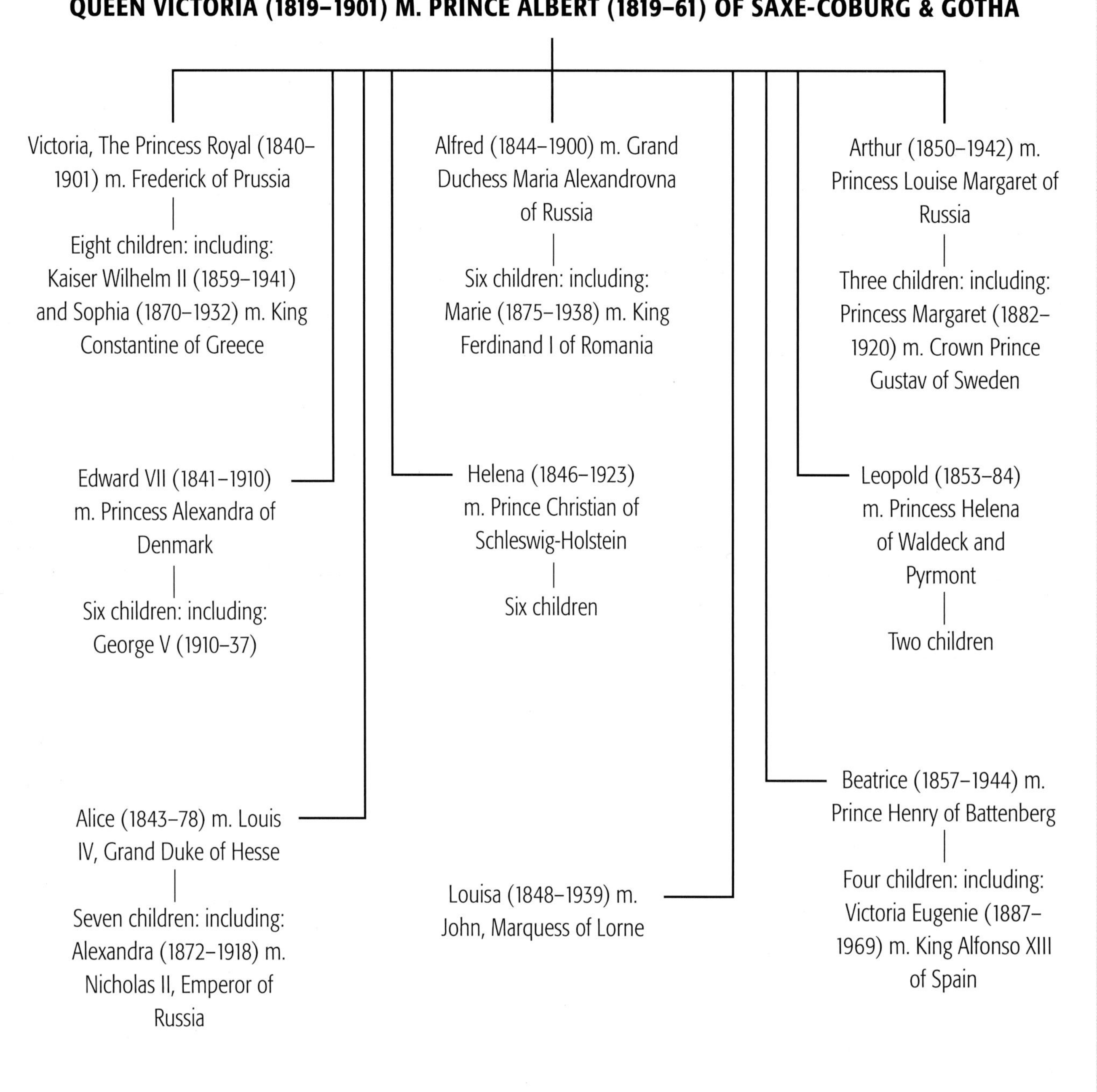

Above: *Queen Victoria's funeral procession travelled from Victoria to Paddington stations. Her body had been transported to London from Osborne House that morning.*

When Victoria died, on the evening of 22 January 1901, the country, literally, came to a standstill. The *London Evening News* had a black-bordered special edition on the street within the hour. People wept openly as the great bell of St Paul's spread the news further, all adults dressed in black, and purple banners were hung from shop windows. Theatrical performances were cancelled, and the mood all over the country was sombre. The queen had requested a full millitary state funeral, which took place on Friday 1 February 1901. The freezing weather did not deter the crowds that turned out to pay their last respects.

Victoria had ruled for 63 years, the longest in British history to date, and most British subjects knew no other monarch. The Britain she left behind at her death was very different from the country at the beginning of her reign. She had presided over a period of unprecedented development in industry and science – innovations including the railways, steam-powered ships, gas lighting, the telephone and major advances in manufacturing methods had ushered in a new era.

The Houses of Saxe-Coburg, Gotha and Windsor
1901–present day

The new century began with a new dynasty: the House of Saxe-Coburg and Gotha. Edward VII was the son of Queen Victoria and Albert, and the German connection created grumblings of public discontent as Europe descended into war; in 1917, his son George V changed the family name to Windsor. Henceforth, the royal family would emphasize that it was British to the core and it played a patriotic role in both world wars. After the Second World War, Elizabeth II developed the role of the monarch as a symbol of the nation. Despite the growth of republican feelings and widely publicized scandals surrounding some members of the family, the monarchy endured, and its reputation revived at the start of the new millennium.

SAXE-COBURG, GOTHA AND WINDSOR MONARCHS

Edward VII (1901–10)
|
George V (1910–36)
|
Edward VIII (1936)
Renounced the crown
|
George VI (1936–52)
|
Elizabeth II (1952–present day)

Edward VII (1901–10)

A popular character, Edward refreshed the monarchy and renewed its high profile. As a young man, Edward – Bertie, as he was known in the family – had enjoyed a self-indulgent life without responsibility: he loved London clubs, going to the races and having affairs with young actresses – both before and after his marriage. From the 1870s, Queen Victoria sent him on various official engagements. He travelled widely, making contacts with the other royal houses of Europe; he or his wife Princess Alexandra of Denmark were related to most of them and he spoke French and German fluently.

As king, Edward was skilful at dealing with ministers and foreign rulers and proved charming at social occasions and

'THERE'LL BE NO WO'AR'

Edward was known for his desire to avoid war in Europe, giving rise to a popular song in in music halls of London's East End:

There'll be no wo'ar
As long as there's a King
like good King Edward.
There'll be no wo'ar
For 'e 'ates that sorta
thing![1]

Above: *This portrait of Edward VII shows the king wearing a field marshal's uniform, the highest rank in the British Army. He wore this outfit for his coronation in Westminster Abbey on 9 August 1902.*

Le Petit Journal

SUPPLÉMENT ILLUSTRÉ

ABONNEMENTS

DIMANCHE 10 MAI 1903

LE ROI D'ANGLETERRE EN FRANCE

Représentation de gala à l'Opéra

Right: *The front cover of this popular Parisian newspaper shows Edward VII attending the Paris Opera during his state visit to France in 1903. Edward was a keen supporter of the arts in Europe.*

ceremonies. Since the role of the monarch was now primarily symbolic, these were important attributes. In general, Edward accepted that he was a constitutional monarch, and that government should rule.

MILITARY AND FOREIGN AFFAIRS

Although acknowledging his purely advisory role, Edward was greatly interested in foreign and military affairs and hoped to have some influence. It is debateable how much impact he had, though. He pushed for Viscount Richard Haldane's reforms of the Army Medical Service and the modernization of the Home Fleet, and opposed cuts in the military budget. But the government was already focused on improving the effectiveness of the army, owing to rising tensions in Europe, so the king's opinions were in line with policy anyway.

Edward wished to help avoid conflict in Europe, although officially he had no diplomatic role. His state visit to France in 1903 clearly promoted goodwill and ameliorated relations between Britain and France, creating an atmosphere that helped enable the Anglo-French Entente Cordiale the following year. He was also involved with achieving the Triple Entente between Britain, France and Russia in 1907. In contrast, the Germans felt that Edward influenced his country against them. Again, the trajectory of British foreign policy was towards alliance with France and Russia and conflict with Germany, so it is hard to ascertain the effect of the king's interventions.

ROYAL PHILANTHROPY

The king and queen embraced the focus on royal philanthropy initiated by Queen Victoria and supported many charities, especially Queen Alexandra. She was glamorous and fashionable but was prepared to meet people in difficulties. She frequently visited the London Hospital and in 1887 she met Joseph Merrick – he had a rare disorder that made his head expand abnormally

and was unkindly nicknamed the 'Elephant Man'. The royal couple visited provincial towns to make the monarchy visible and develop good public relations, which became vital for the survival of the institution.

Above: *Queen Alexandra's first public act, the Reception of the Queen Victoria's Institute of Nurses by Her Majesty at Marlborough House on 3 July 1901. This image of Edward VII's wife helped to cement the monarchy's commitment to philanthropy. It first appeared in* The Illustrated London News *on 13 July. 1901.*

Opposite: *King George V and Queen Mary attending the third opening of Parliament after the coronation. Mary is wearing her coronation gown.*

GEORGE V (1910–36)

Although several European monarchies collapsed as a result of the First World War, the British royal family was strengthened during George V's reign. Initially destined for a naval life, George was catapulted to the succession on the death of his older brother. In contrast to his father, he led a virtuous married life and preferred spending time in the English countryside to travel. He made the royal estate of Sandringham in Norfolk his home and was fond of shooting.

CONSTITUTIONAL CRISIS

George V's skills as a constitutional monarch were tested from the start. The House of Lords had rejected the radical Liberal government's budget of 1909, which proposed a tax on unearned income. Prime Minister Henry Asquith intended to restrict the power of the House of Lords and introduced the Parliament Bill to prevent the Lords from vetoing any measure passed by the Commons. Unwilling to lose influence, the House of Lords refused to pass this bill. Asquith asked George to create sufficient Liberal peers to prevent Conservative opposition to the bill in the House of Lords; the king had the power to create peers, but the prime minister decided who should receive the honour. The king felt uncomfortable being put under pressure to create peers. However, after the second election of the year in November 1910, won by the Liberals once again, he submitted to Asquith's request. In the event, the House of Lords passed the Parliament Bill in 1911 without the introduction of new peers – they did not want the House to be filled with Liberals.

THE FIRST WORLD WAR

In 1908, George had visited Berlin in an attempt to reduce tension with Germany, but his mission had failed. When war broke out in 1914, the German background of the royal family came under fire. The author H. G. Wells called for end to the 'alien and uninspiring court', to which the king responded: 'I may be uninspiring but I'll be damned if I'm an alien.'[2] George backed the war effort by wearing military uniform; adopting a frugal lifestyle; and making more than 450 visits to troops and 300 hospital visits to injured servicemen. His actions went down well with the public.

As a result of the war, the German, Austro-Hungarian and Russian monarchies collapsed, but the prestige of the monarchy grew in Britain, where it was perceived

Below: *British troops enthusiastically welcoming King George V during one of his many visits to the front line during the First World War. His wartime support of workers in hospitals, factories and dockyards garnered him much praise from the public.*

REJECTING THE ROMANOVS

George V and Prime Minister Lloyd George had initially supported giving asylum to the Russian royal family, but growing anti-royalist feelings in Britain after the Russian Revolution led the king to change his mind. George instructed his private secretary Lord Stanfordham to write to Foreign Secretary Arthur Balfour on 6 April 1917: 'Every day the King is becoming more concerned about the question of the Emperor and Empress of Russia coming to this country.' A second letter that day stated: 'There is evidence in this country of the ex-Emperor and Empress coming to this country would be resented by the public. The opposition to them coming here is so strong that we must be allowed to withdraw from the consent previously given to the Russian government's proposal.'[3] In 1918, the Bolshevik government executed Tsar Nicholas and his family.

Left: *Tsar Nicholas II, the last emperor of Russia, pictured in captivity with his daughters before execution.*

as a symbol of continuity in turbulent times. The British monarchy was constitutional rather than autocratic, and the royal family declared that it had nothing to do with the unreformed monarchies. When the Russian Tsar was overthrown by revolution in 1917, George refused to give asylum to the Russian royal family, even though Tsar Nicholas II was his cousin. After the war, the Windsors had to remain staunchly British – rather than intermarrying with European royalty, family members mostly married British spouses.

THE KING AS MEDIATOR

In domestic politics, King George followed his brief to take a neutral position. He was responsible for calling on ministers to form a government, but he always sought advice from leading politicians. In 1923, he chose Stanley Baldwin to be the Conservative prime minister. In a second election later that year, a hung Parliament resulted. The Conservatives were the largest party, but the Liberals would not work with them. Although he did not agree with Labour, the second largest party, he invited Ramsay MacDonald in 1924 to form a minority Labour government; constitutionally, it was the correct decision. And he made the effort to get on with MacDonald. In the wake of the 1929 Great Depression, which had a disastrous effect on the economy, George was involved in persuading MacDonald not to resign and instead to form a National Coalition government with Baldwin and the Liberal leader Sir Herbert Samuel. In 1931, this coalition under MacDonald won the general election.

COLONIES AND DOMINIONS

The relationship between Britain and its dominions changed with the 1931 Statute of Westminster. The dominions were the European-ruled colonies, including the Irish Free State, Canada, Australia and South Africa, which had been allowed to run their internal affairs. They were now to be regarded as 'autonomous communities' within the British Empire, equal in status to Britain. The status of other colonies in Asia and Africa remained unchanged. Interestingly, the Statute gave more power to the monarch. The dominions were no longer controlled by Parliament, but they retained their allegiance to the Crown. The position of Head of the Dominions, later the Commonwealth (see page 181), became one of the most important roles of the monarch in the 20th century.

EDWARD VIII (JANUARY–DECEMBER 1936)

Edward VIII renounced his Crown to marry Wallis Simpson, the only British monarch to abdicate voluntarily. Perhaps the first royal celebrity, Edward was young, attractive and fashionable, with a magnetic personality. He met Mrs Wallis Simpson in 1931 and after she divorced her husband in 1936, Edward wanted to marry her. The government opposed the union. The king was Head of the Church, but official Church doctrine opposed divorce; marriage to a divorcee would have raised questions about the king's relations with the Church and proved unacceptable to the public. England did not recognize morganatic marriage, where the spouse did not take on the title or privileges of the monarch. Edward had to choose between the monarchy and marriage – and he chose Wallis Simpson. In December 1936, Edward abdicated in favour of his younger brother. He married the love of his life and they left the country.

Below: *King Edward VIII and Mrs Wallis Simpson on holiday in Yugoslavia during the summer of 1936. After one of the shortest reigns in British history (just under 12 months), Edward abdicated and departed for Austria the following day.*

WAS EDWARD A NAZI SYMPATHIZER?

In 1937, Edward and Mrs Simpson made a controversial visit to Germany, where they met with Nazi leaders and Edward expressed great admiration for Adolf Hitler. Many have alleged he was a potential or even an active traitor. According to historian A. W. Purdue, at the very least, Edward craved to feel important again, and in Germany the couple were welcomed as distinguished visitors. Whatever his views, the former king's behaviour proved an embarrassment when Britain went to war with Germany, and he was swiftly moved away from Europe to become Governor of the Bahamas.

GEORGE VI 1936–52

As the younger brother of Edward VIII, Albert – as he was originally called – was unprepared for kingship. But with the devoted assistance of his wife, Elizabeth, George VI overcame poor health and a debilitating stammer to earn his subjects' respect, support the government and people during the Second World War, and keep the institution of monarchy secure.

A WARTIME MONARCH

In the 1930s, George had hoped to prevent the slide towards war. He offered to contact the leaders of the Axis powers Adolf Hitler, Benito Mussolini and Emperor Hirohito directly, but the government rejected the proposal. Although the king could not affect policy, he expected to be consulted, and was involved in calling on Winston Churchill to replace Neville Chamberlain as prime minister in 1940 when it became apparent that Chamberlain was an ineffective wartime leader. The king became a close confidant of Churchill's during the war. George gave his unwavering support on the

Above: *King George VI making his historical broadcast to the nation on his Coronation Day, 12 May 1937.*

Right: *Prime Minister Winston Churchill in 1941. His parliamentary speeches galvanized support for the war effort.*

THE KING'S SPEECH

This 2010 film tells the true story of how the king overcame his stammer with the help of Australian speech therapist Lionel Logue. A special friendship blossomed between the king and the commoner, as George learnt to speak confidently. The king's first radio speech was broadcast to rally the nation at the outbreak of war on 3 September 1939. It began:

> *In this grave hour, perhaps the most fateful in our history, I send to every household of my peoples, both at home and overseas, this message, with the same depth of feeling for each one of you as if I were able to cross your threshold and speak to you myself. For the second time in the lives of most of us we are at War.*[4]

Home Front. Against political advice, he declared that the royal family would remain in London during the Blitz of 1940–41 to show solidarity with Londoners. They stayed in Buckingham Palace, which was bombed nine times – luckily, no one in the family was injured. His daughter, Princess Elizabeth, also played her part, training as a driver in the Women's Auxiliary Territory Service (WATS). George visited bombed areas in the East End and in other cities following air raids, and broadcast messages to promote the war effort. He also travelled to France in 1939 to offer encouragement to the British Expeditionary Force and to North Africa in 1943 after the Allied victory at El Alamein. Ten days after the D-Day landings of June 1944, George was on the beaches of Normandy. Although Churchill was always in charge, the king symbolized the nation in wartime.

In recognition of the king's wartime functions, Buckingham Palace was a focus for the Victory in Europe celebrations on 8 May 1945. The royal family was heartily cheered by the crowds – a high point for the 20th-century monarchy.

Opposite: *King George VI inspecting the lightweight compact rations that were designed to provide a balanced diet for airborne troops. He and his wife Queen Elizabeth provided much-needed moral support throughout the war years.*

HEAD OF THE COMMONWEALTH

George was privately disappointed when Churchill lost the general election in 1945 and unhappy about the incoming Labour government. Yet he did his duty, developing amicable relations with Prime Minister Clement Atlee. Under Labour, the British Empire was dismantled, and Asian and African colonies gained their independence. From 1947, the monarch was no longer the Emperor of India. The former colonies joined the Commonwealth of Nations; from 1949, the British monarch became the Head of the Commonwealth. The king accepted decolonization and the adjustment to his symbolic role.

TOURING SOUTHERN AFRICA

In 1947, George, Elizabeth and their young daughters went on a family tour of South Africa to strengthen the links with this Commonwealth country. They travelled around meeting and greeting local people, exchanging handshakes as little girls curtseyed and presented bouquets of flowers to the royal party. Sarah Gertrude Millin, author and biographer of South African Prime Minister Jan Smuts, described how the visit 'sweetened the atmosphere of South Africa. Here came four Royal people from England – and they were… modest, lovable, so anxious to please, so eagerly pleased, that it was almost painful to watch them doing their duty.'[5]

Right: *Princess Elizabeth's first overseas trip, aged 21. Here she is speaking to a local mayor at St George's Park in Port Elizabeth during her tour of South Africa in 1947.*

ELIZABETH II (1952–PRESENT DAY)

Opposite: *The coronation of Elizabeth II in Westminster Abbey, London, 2 June 1953. Elizabeth was crowned with St Edward's Crown, which was made of solid gold in 1661.*

Britain's longest-reigning monarch, Elizabeth II has upheld her constitutional role. From the moment of her accession, the young queen understood the importance of managing the media. In post-war austerity Britain, her coronation provided some longed-for glamour – tens of thousands of cheering spectators witnessed the royal procession to Westminster Abbey. Against the wishes of Prime Minister Churchill, Elizabeth had insisted that the coronation service be televised, and many citizens bought their first TV set especially for the occasion. The coronation and public celebrations were broadcast on radio and TV across the UK, the Commonwealth and the rest of the world.

ROYAL PREROGATIVE

The queen retains the royal prerogative to call on politicians to form a government, after consultation with senior leaders. In the 1950s and early 1960s, she played a role in appointing the prime minister because the Conservative Party lacked a process for choosing its leader. When the Conservative Prime Minister Anthony Eden resigned 1957, Elizabeth consulted with the Cabinet and appointed Harold Macmillan rather than R. A. Butler. In 1963, when Harold Macmillan resigned, she followed Macmillan's advice and asked Lord Home to become the prime minister. To avoid this issue from recurring, the Conservative Party adopted a formal procedure in 1965 for electing its leader so it was no longer the queen's responsibility to ask a Conservative politician to form a government. Yet if Parliament has no overall majority, the queen still has the prerogative – with advice from the Cabinet – to appoint the prime minister. In 1974, she sent for Harold Wilson to take up the post.

'ROYAL FAMILY'

In this BBC documentary, which was watched by an estimated three-quarters of the population, the queen was shown carrying out official duties as well as relaxing in her royal residences and celebrating Christmas with her family. The nation discovered that she stored leftover food in Tupperware containers, just like ordinary people. It was an excellent public relations exercise, but Princess Anne detested the intrusion of the film: 'I thought it was a rotten idea. The attention which had been brought upon one ever since one was a child… you just didn't need any more.'[6]

Above: *A camera films Queen Elizabeth II and her family at breakfast for the 1969 documentary 'Royal Family'.*

In the late 1950s, opposition to the monarchy arose; it was criticized as an obstacle to modernization. The backlash continued into the 1960s, when a movement for social change questioned the monarchy's consumption of resources and whether it was needed at all. The queen's solution was to continue with her duties and let in the cameras to promote the family and ceremonial aspects of the monarchy. In 1969, she sanctioned the BBC programme 'Royal Family', a detailed documentary that provided a window into the lives of the Windsors. In 1970, the queen invented the royal 'walkabout' and started meeting local people as well as officials when she went on tours. To reinforce the ceremonial side, her jubilees became major celebrations. For her Silver Jubilee in 1977, people across the UK held street parties. But backing for the monarchy was still contested. That year, the Sex Pistols' anti-royalist song 'God Save the Queen' rose high in the music charts.

Opposite: *The wedding of Prince Charles and Princess Diana in 1981. The event received a TV audience of approximately 750 million.*

The royal family lived increasingly in the public eye. The press intruded into their lives, claiming that disclosures about the monarchy were in the public interest and giving them disproportionate attention. The media focused on the young women and they became celebrities, their lives portrayed as a royal soap opera. Princess Diana, married to Prince Charles in a fairy-tale wedding in 1981, was particularly popular. Attractive and stylish, she became associated with diverse charitable causes, including controversial campaigns to support the victims of AIDS and landmines.

THE *ANNUS HORRIBILIS*

Living under the media spotlight, members of the royal family were expected to have higher standards of behaviour than the general public, but they struggled to live up to the ideal. The queen looked back on 1992 as her *annus horribilis* – horrible year. Firstly, three of her children were in the limelight for negative reasons. Charles and Diana separated, as did Prince Andrew from Sarah Ferguson, and Princess Anne got divorced. The press printed lurid revelations, and the couples were constantly in the news. The royal family was no longer seen as a model family, and loyalty to the monarchy declined. To cap it all, a huge fire swept through Windsor Castle towards the end of year. It was not insured, which led to a row about who would fund the £40 million cost of refurbishment. Many people had been asking why the queen did not

Below: *On 20 November 1992, fire swept through Windsor Castle causing extensive damage to over 100 rooms.*

pay tax like everyone else; that year, she finally agreed to start paying income and capital gains tax. In 1993, Buckingham Palace was opened to the public to provide income to help finance the cost of restoring Windsor Castle.

REACTION AND REVIVAL

The reaction against the royal family deepened in the late 1990s when Prince Charles and Princess Diana divorced in 1996. The scandal-mongering press leapt on the relationship between Prince Charles and Camilla Parker Bowles, which had developed while Charles was still married, and after the royal divorce, the romance between Princess Diana and Dodi Fayed, son of the Egyptian business magnate Mohammed Al-Fayed. In 1997, Diana and Dodi Fayed were killed in a car crash in Paris while being chased by paparazzi. The tragic accident led to a widespread outpouring of grief over the princess's death, which the royal family had not anticipated. The queen was criticized in the press for her misjudgement in not responding sufficiently to the strong public reaction – the monarchy was perceived as out of touch with ordinary people.

Below: *The sea of flowers in front of Kensington Palace following the death of Princess Diana in 1997. Diana was widely mourned, and her funeral was broadcast in 200 countries.*

Above: *Queen Elizabeth II on a royal visit to Berlin in 2015.*

Above right: *Prince William, Kate Middleton, Meghan Markle and Prince Harry attend a service on Christmas Day 2018.*

Elizabeth rode out the storm and continued her public-relations efforts, travelling regularly in the UK and Commonwealth countries, and offering patronage to charities and cultural institutions. The early 2000s saw a revival in the popularity of the monarchy. To celebrate her Diamond Jubilee in 2012, the queen toured the UK over several months. Her approval rating rose to 90 per cent – the highest since her accession to the throne.

Prince Charles and Princess Diana's sons William and Harry, with their modernizing influence, contributed to the rising approval of the monarchy. William married Catherine Middleton in 2011 – she was the first royal bride with a university degree. After her marriage, she gave up paid work and focused on championing children's mental health. Prince Harry's marriage to the Hollywood actress Meghan Markle in 2018 proved more controversial; she became the first black member of the British royal family. The marriage indicated the ability of the institution of monarchy to evolve and adapt to changing circumstances to ensure its survival.

MODERNIZING THE RULES

In 2013, the Succession to the Crown Act overturned male primogeniture. The eldest child of the monarch could succeed to the throne regardless of gender. It also removed the disqualification from the succession arising from marrying a Catholic.

CHAPTER NOTES

CHAPTER 1

[1] Morton, 35 and https://en.wikisource.org/wiki/Page:The_Anglo-Saxon_Chronicle_(Giles).djvu/81

[2] https://www.royal.uk/alfred-great-r-871-899, from Laws of Alfred, c.885-99

[3] Edward the Elder, 899-924, edited by N. J. Higham, David Hill, p2

[4] Morton, 37

[5] https://www.historytoday.com/richard-cavendish/archbishop-aelfheah-canterbury-murdered-vikings

[6] Loades, 38 and https://en.wikisource.org/wiki/The_Anglo-Saxon_Chronicle_(Giles)

[7] https://en.wikisource.org/wiki/The_Anglo-Saxon_Chronicle_(Giles)

[8] Loades, 54 and Ormrod, 50

CHAPTER 2

[1] Delderfield, 21, from the Anglo-Saxon Chronicle

[2] http://www.bbc.co.uk/history/british/normans/bayeux_tapestry_gallery_02.shtml, from the Anglo-Saxon Chronicle

[3] https://www.bbc.com/timelines/zp88wmn#ztsy34j

[4] https://books.google.co.uk/books?id=tPF4DwAAQBAJ&pg=PT41&lpg=PT41&dq=

[5] Loades, 71

[6] http://www.englishmonarchs.co.uk/normans_2.htm and Ormrod, 66

[7] David Bates in Ormrod, 77

CHAPTER 3

[1] http://www.owain-glyndwr.wales/age_of_the_princes/summary4.html

[2] http://www.greghill.cymru/elegy-for-llywelyn-ap-gruffudd.html

CHAPTER 4

[1] http://www.oxforddnb.com/abstract/10.1093/ref:odnb/9780198614128.001.0001/odnb-9780198614128-e-12949?rskey=6d6HR2&result=3

[2] https://plato.stanford.edu/entries/john-salisbury/church.html

[3] https://doi.org/10.1093/ref:odnb/23498, quote from Crusade of Richard Lionheart

[4] https://sourcebooks.fordham.edu/basis/williamofnewburgh-four.asp#10

[5] https://doi.org/10.1093/ref:odnb/14841, quote from contemporary historian Roger of Howden

[6] Ormrod, 121

[7] Ormrod, 123

[8] Briggs, 68

[9] https://epistolae.ctl.columbia.edu/letter/648.html

[10] https://www.pressreader.com/uk/bbc-history-magazine/20160519/282750586026835

CHAPTER 5

[1] https://www.bbc.co.uk/history/scottishhistory/darkages/features_darkages_constantine2.shtml

[2] https://doi.org/10.1093/ref:odnb/18044

[3] https://www.bbc.co.uk/history/scottishhistory/independence/intro_independence2.shtml

[4] http://www.bbc.co.uk/scotland/history/articles/william_wallace/, quote from Scotichronicon

[5] https://www.oxforddnb.com/view/10.1093/ref:odnb/9780198614128.001.0001/odnb-9780198614128-e-23713#odnb-9780198614128-e-23713

CHAPTER 6

[1] http://www.castlewales.com/jsgeorge.html

[2] Morton, 78

[3] https://doi.org/10.1093/ref:odnb/8518

[4] http://www.eyewitnesstohistory.com/plague.htm

[5] Morton, 95

[6] https://sourcebooks.fordham.edu/source/anon1381.asp

[7] https://doi.org/10.1093/ref:odnb/23499

CHAPTER 7

[1] From a speech given by Henry IV, 1399, https://doi.org/10.1093/ref:odnb/12951

[2] http://www.eyewitnesstohistory.com/agincourt.htm

[3] http://www.oxforddnb.com/view/10.1093/ref:odnb/9780198614128.001.0001/odnb-9780198614128-e-12953?rskey=aJWL5n&result=3#odnb-9780198614128-e-12953-div1-d6905e1124

[4] https://warfarehistorynetwork.com/daily/military-history/red-storm-rising/

[5] https://thehistoryofengland.co.uk/resource/crowland-chronicle/

[6] Loades, 218 and https://library.eb.co.uk/levels/adult/article/Richard-III/63548

[7] Ormrod, 188

[8] www.blancheparry.com/articles/who-killed-king-richard-III.pdf

CHAPTER 8

[1] https://www.bartleby.com/209/245.html#note245.1

[2] https://www.bartleby.com/209/51.html

[3] Scarisbrick, Henry VIII, 526, cited in https://doi.org/10.1093/ref:odnb/12955

[4] http://www.tudorplace.com.ar/Bios/ElizabethBarton.htm

[5] https://library.eb.co.uk/levels/adult/article/Thomas-More/53689#5009.toc

[6] Quoted from State Papers, Henry VIII, 2.538, https://doi.org/10.1093/ref:odnb/12955

[7] https://www.canterbury.ac.nz/exhibition/kjb/bible_in_english/Reformation.shtml

[8] https://doi.org/10.1093/ref:odnb/8522

[9] Loades, 250

[10] https://www.royal.uk/edward-vi

[11] From Foxe's Book of Martyrs by John Milner, 1925–6, https://archive.org/details

[12] http://www.luminarium.org/renlit/elizlet5.htm

[13] https://sourcebooks.fordham.edu/mod/elizabeth1.asp and http://www.luminarium.org/renlit/elizspeechreligion.htm

[14] http://www.shakespeare-online.com/biography/patronelizabeth.html

[15] http://www.nationalarchives.gov.uk/education/resources/elizabeth-monarchy/sir-francis-drake-to-elizabeth/

CHAPTER 9

[1] http://www.bbc.co.uk/history/scottishhistory/renaissance/features_renaissance_mary.shtml

[2] https://medium.com/there-shall-be-an-independent-scotland/facing-the-rascal-multitude-john-knox-may-11th-and-perths-revolutionary-reformation-2e269e3c7ba5

CHAPTER 10

[1] http://www.constitution.org/eng/petright.htm

[2] https://www.britannica.com/biography/William-Lenthall

[3] https://library.eb.co.uk/levels/adult/article/United-Kingdom/110750#44864.toc

[4] http://www.bbc.co.uk/history/british/civil_war_revolution/benn_levellers_01.shtml

[5] John Morrill, 2011, 'Oliver Cromwell', BBC History http://www.bbc.co.uk/history/british/civil_war_revolution/cromwell_01.shtml

[6] https://www.pepysdiary.com/diary/1666/09/

[7] Ormrod, 249

[8] https://www.irishcentral.com/news/catholic-irish-soldiers-battle-boyne

[9] http://avalon.law.yale.edu/17th_century/england.asp

[10] https://www.royal.uk/william-and-mary

CHAPTER 11

[1] https://library.eb.co.uk/levels/adult/article/Act-of-Settlement/66926

[2] http://www.bbc.co.uk/arts/robertburns/works/therell_never_be_peace_till_jamie_comes_hame/ and http://www.rampantscotland.com/songs/blsongs_jamie.htm

[3] http://www.tartansauthority.com/tartan/the-growth-of-tartan/The-Batle-of-Culloden/eye-witness-account

[4] Letter pdf on https://www.royal.uk/george-iii

[5] https://austenonly.com/2012/05/30/george-iiis-golden-jubilee/

[6] https://www.royal.uk/william-iv

[7] https://www.royal.uk/queen-victoria Diary extracts

[8] https://library.eb.co.uk/levels/adult/article/Victoria/108774

[9] https://www.royal.uk/queen-victoria Diary extracts

[10] Ormrod, 300

CHAPTER 12

[1] Juliet Nicolson (2008),The Perfect Summer: England 1911, p.57

[2] Ormrod, 308

[3] http://dianalegacy.com/royal-scandal-king-george-v-ruthlessly-knifed-tsar-nicholas-in-back-to-save-royal-family/

[4] https://www.coursehero.com/file/25360397/Analysis-of-King-Georges-VI-Speech/

[5] http://www.theheritageportal.co.za/article/rediscovering-1947-royal-visit-south-africa

[6] http://royalcentral.co.uk/blogs/whatever-happened-to-the-1969-film-royal-family-5279

INDEX

Aelfheah, Archbishop 15, 18, 19
Aethelbald 9
Aethelberht 9
Aethelflaed 13
Aetheling, Edgar 24
Aethelred I 9, 13
Aethelred II (the Unready) 9, 15, 16, 17, 18, 19
Aetheling, Edgar 31
Aetheling, William 33
Aethelwulf 9
Agincourt, Battle of 82, 84
Albert, Prince 164, 165, 166, 167, 170, 172
Alexander I 56
Alexander II 56
Alexander III 56, 61
Alexandra of Denmark 172, 173-4
Alfred the Great 9, 10, 12
American War of Independence 155-6
Andrew, Prince 185
Anglo-Saxon Chronicle 12, 15, 17, 20, 28, 29, 57
Anne I 128, 146, 147
Anne, Princess 182, 185
Anne of Cleves 105
Anonimalle Chronicle 77
Anselm 29, 31, 32
Argyll, Duke of 141
Ashdown, Battle of 10
Asquith, Henry 176
Athelstan 9, 14, 15, 57
Atlee, Clement 181

Babington, Henry 116
Bacon, Francis 96, 118, 131
Bagehot, Walter 168
Baldwin, Stanley 177
Balfour, Arthur 177
Balliol, Edward 56, 64-5
Balliol, John 56, 61, 62
Bane, Donald 56
Bannockburn, Battle of 64, 71
Barlow, Frank 20
Barton, Elizabeth 103
Bates, David 30
Bayeux Tapestry 20-1, 24
Beatrice, Princess 189
Becket, Thomas à 44-5
Bennett, Alan 157
Berwick, Battle of 62, 63
Black Death 74-5
Boccaccio, Giovanni 74
Boleyn, Anne 102, 103, 105, 115
Bolingbroke, Henry 78-9
Bonaparte, Napoleon 157-8
Bonner, Bishop 112
Book of Martyrs (Foxe) 112
Bosworth Field, Battle of 93
Bower, Walter 63
Boyne, Battle of the 143, 144
British Empire 168, 177, 181
Bruce, Marjorie 65
Bruce, Robert 61, 66
Brunanburh, Battle of 57, 58
Buckingham, Duke of 132
Burns, Robert 150
Butler, Eleanor 91
Bulter, R.A. 182
Byrhtnoth 17

Calvin, John 127
Carteret, John 151-2
Catesby, Robert 130
Catherine of Aragon 99, 100, 101, 103, 105
Catherine of Valois 84
Cecil, William 115
Chamberlain, Neville 179
Charles, Prince 184, 185, 186, 188
Charles I 128, 132-7, 141
Charles I d'Albret 84
Charles II 128, 137, 138-41
Charles V (King of France) 73, 99
Charles VI (King of France) 80, 84
Charter of Liberties 30-1
Church, S. D. 51
Churchill, Winston 179, 181, 182
Clive, Robert 153
Cnut 9, 12, 18
Commonwealth 177, 181
Concordat of London 32
Confirmation of the Charters 70
Constantine I 56
Constantine II 13, 56, 57, 58
Constantine III 56
Cranmer, Thomas 101, 103, 107, 112
Crécy, Battle of 73, 74
Cromwell, Oliver 136, 137
Cromwell, Thomas 101
Crowland Chronicles 88
Crusades 46, 48
Culloden, Battle of 152
Curthose, Robert 31
Danelaw 8, 10, 11
Darnley, Lord 127
David I 56, 59
David II 56, 64-5
de la Pole, Michael 78
de la Pole, William 85
de Montfort, Simon 53, 55, 68
Declaration of Rights 144, 145
Despenser, Hugh 71
Dettingen, Battle of 152
Diana, Princess 184, 185, 186
Disraeli, Benjamin 167
Domesday Book 28
Donald, Earl of Mar 65
Donald I 56
Donald II 56
Drake, Francis 120, 121
Dudley, Guilford 110
Dudley, John 107, 108
Dudley, Robert 115
Duncan I 56
Dunnottar, Battle of 58
Dupplin Moor, Battle of 65

Eadred 9
Eadwig 9, 18
Eden, Anthony 182
Edgar (King of England) 9
Edgar (King of Scotland) 56
Edington, Battle of 10
Edmund, Prince 53
Edmund I 9
Edmund II (Ironside) 9, 18
Edward the Confessor 9, 12, 19-21, 22
Edward the Elder 9, 13, 15
Edward the Martyr 9, 15
Edward I 37, 55, 61-2, 63, 64, 66, 67-8, 70
Edward II 64, 66, 70-3
Edward III 64, 65, 66, 73-5
Edward IV 80, 86, 88-90, 125
Edward V 80, 90, 91
Edward VI 94, 107-10
Edward VII 167, 172-4
Edward VIII 172, 178
Egbert 9
Eleanor of Aquitaine 33, 45, 46
Eleanor of Provence 53, 55
Elizabeth I 94, 109, 114-21, 126, 127
Elizabeth II 172, 181, 182-9
Elizabeth, Queen Mother 179
Emma of Normandy 19
English Constitution, The (Bagehot) 168
Eugenie, Princess 189
Falkirk, Battle of 66
Fawkes, Guy 130
Fayed, Dodi 186
Ferguson, Sarah 185
feudalism 22, 25, 26, 59-60
First World War 176-7
Fisher, John 96
Forkbeard, Svein 9, 17-18
Foxe, John 112
François II 125, 127
Frederick (King of Bohemia) 131

Gaveston, Piers 70, 71
George I 148-51
George II 148, 151-3
George III 148, 154-8
George IV 148, 157, 159
George V 172, 174-7
George VI 172, 178, 179-81
Girth 24
Glorious Revolution 143
Glyndwr, Owain 38, 39, 40, 80-1
Godwine, Earl of Wessex 19
Great Exhibition 166, 167
Great Fire of London 140
Greville, Charles 164
Grey, Lady Jane 109-10
Grey, Lord 161
Gruffudd ap Cynan 34
Gruffudd ap Llywelyn 34, 36
Gunpowder Plot 130
Gwynedd, Owain 34

Haldane, Richard 173
Hardecanute 9
Harold I (Harefoot) 9
Harold II 9, 19, 22, 24, 36
Harry, Prince 187
Hastings, Battle of 22, 24
Hawkins, John 121
Henry I 22, 30-2, 42
Henry II 33, 42, 43-5
Henry III 37, 42, 53-5, 68, 80
Henry IV 38, 78-9, 80-2
Henry V 38, 80, 82-4
Henry V, Emperor 32-3
Henry VI 80, 85-6, 88
Henry VI (Holy Roman Emperor) 46
Henry VII 40, 93, 94-7
Henry VIII 41, 94, 97-106, 109, 110
Hepburn, James 127
Hirohito, Emperor 179
Hitler, Adolf 178, 179
Hotspur's Rebellion 82

Howard, Catherine 105
Hundred Years' War 73, 82, 84, 85-6
Hywel Dda the Good 34, 36, 37

Ireland 78, 117, 134, 136, 141, 143

Jacobites 148, 150, 151
James I (King of Scotland) 65, 122, 124
James I/VI 121, 122, 127, 128-31
James II 128, 141-4, 146, 148
James II (King of Scotland) 122
James III (King of Scotland) 122, 124
James IV (King of Scotland) 122, 123, 124
James V (King of Scotland) 122, 124, 125
Jewish population 49
Joan of Arc 86
John 42, 46, 50-52
John of Gaunt 75, 78-9
John of Salisbury 45
Jordon, Dorothea 161

Kenneth III 56
Kett's Rebellion 108
Knox, John 115, 126

Laud, William 134, 135
Lentall, William 135
Leofwin 24
Levellers 136, 137
Lewes, Battle of 55
Liverpool, Lord 159
Lloyd George, David 177
Llywelyn ap Gruffudd the Last 34, 37, 40
Llywelyn ap Iorwerth the Great 34
Logue, Lionel 179
Lollards 82
London 12, 140
Louis VI 31
Louis VII 45
Louis VIII 53
Louis XI 88
Louis XIV 140

MacAlpin, Kenneth 56, 57, 64
Macbeth 56
MacDonald, Ramsay 177
Macmillan, Harold 182
Magna Carta 30-1, 42, 50, 51, 52, 70
Malcolm I 56
Malcolm II 56
Malcolm III 24, 31, 56, 59
Malcolm IV 56
Maldon, Battle of 17
Margaret of Anjou 86
Margaret, Maid of Norway 56, 61
Margaret of Scotland, Saint 59, 60
Maria, Henrietta 132
Markle, Meghan 187
Marston Moor, Battle of 136
Mary I 94, 109, 110-13
Mary II 128, 140, 143, 144-6
Mary of Guise 125-6
Mary, Queen of Scots 116, 117, 122, 125, 127
Matilda 31, 32, 33, 42
Mawr, Rhodri 34, 36
Melbourne, Lord 161, 164
Merrick, Joseph 173-4
Middleton, Catherine 187
Millin, Sarah Gertrude 181
Monmouth, Duke of 141
Monteagle, Lord 130
More, Thomas 101, 104
Murray, Andrew 62, 65
Mussolini, Benito 179

Napoleonic Wars 157-8
Naseby, Battle of 136
Nelson, Horatio 158
New Forest 26
New Ordinances 70-1
Nicholas II, Tsar 177
Nine Years' War 146
North, Lord 156

Offa 34
Oliver, Neil 58
O'Neill, Hugh 117
Orm 36
Osborne, Thomas 140

Parker Bowles, Camilla 186
Parr, Catherine 105
Paschal II, Pope 32
Peasant's Revolt 76-7
Peel, Robert 164
Pepys, Samuel 140
Percy, Henry 'Hotspur' 82
Petition of the Barons 53
Petition of Right 134
Philip II (King of France) 46, 50
Philip II (King of Spain) 113, 115, 119
Philip IV 68
Philip VI 65
Philip Augustus (France) 43, 45
Philippe I 26
Pilgrimage of Grace 106
Pitt the Younger 156, 157
Provisions of Oxford 53
Pym, John 135

Reform Act (1832) 161
Richard of York 86
Richard I 42, 45, 46-8
Richard II 38, 66, 76-9, 80
Richard III 80
Robert I (the Bruce) 56, 64, 65, 71
Robert II 56, 65
Robert III 56, 65, 82, 91, 92, 93
Robert, Duke of Albany 65
Robert, Earl of Gloucester 33
Royal Family 182, 185

Salah ad-Din 48
Samuel, Herbert 177
Scotland 13, 15, 24, 28, 29, 56-65, 66, 68, 73, 81, 101, 116, 122-7, 134, 136, 141, 146, 188
Second World War 179-81
Seven Years' War 153
Seymour, Edward 107, 108-9
Seymour, Jane 105
Shakespeare, William 118
Shrewsbury, Battle of 82
Simpson, Wallis 178
South Sea Bubble 150-1
Spanish Armada 119-20
Spenser, Edmund 118
Stamford Bridge, Battle of 24
Stanfordham, Lord 177
Stanhope, James 150
Stanley, Thomas 93
Statute of Labourers 75
Stephen 22, 32-3, 43
Stevens, John 144
Stewart, Murdoch 65
Stirling Bridge, Battle of 62
Stone of Destiny 62, 64
Strafford, Earl of 135
Stuart, Charles Edward (Bonnie Prince Charlie) 151, 152
Stuart, James Edward 150, 151, 152
Sunderland, Charles 150

Tettenhall, Battle of 13
Tewkesbury, Battle of 86
Theobald, Archbishop 45
Thirty Years' War 131, 132
Thomas of Lancaster 71
Tirel, Walter 31
Trafalgar, Battle of 158
Tryggvason, Olaf 15, 17
Tyler, Wat 76, 77

Urban II, Pope 29

Victoria 148, 162-71, 172
Vincent, Nicholas 55

Wakefield, Battle of 86
Wales 28, 29, 34-41, 66, 80-1
Wallace, William 62, 63, 66
Walpole, Robert 150-2
Walter, Hubert 46
War of the Austrian Succession 152
Warbeck, Perkin 94
Wars of the Roses 40, 85, 86, 93, 94
Waterloo, Battle of 158
Wavrin, Jehan de 84
Wellington, Lord 159
Wells, H.G. 176
White Ship 33
William, Prince 187
William I 19, 22, 23-6, 28, 59
William I the Lion 56
William II 22, 28-9, 31
William III 128, 140, 143, 144-6
William IV 148, 160-2
William of Malmesbury 13, 31
William of Newburgh 49
Wilson, Harold 182
Wolsey, Thomas 97, 99, 105
Woodville, Elizabeth 91
Wycliffe, John 82

Picture Credits

t = top, b = bottom, r = right, l = left, c = centre

Alamy: 13t, 13b, 23, 27, 34, 36, 39, 46, 48, 55, 82, 97b, 108t, 109, 126b, 139, 146, 164b, 177, 186, 187r

Bridgeman Images: 8, 17t, 33r, 40, 43, 72, 78, 81, 90, 91, 96, 105t, 106, 113, 135, 143, 165, 169, 174, 176

British Library: 31b, 71

British Museum: 63t

Getty Images: 61, 64, 67, 69, 70, 86b, 105cr, 117, 118, 153, 171, 175, 179t, 179b, 181, 182, 183, 184, 185, 188-9

Lovell Johns: 11, 35

Metropolitan Museum of Art: 156b

Shutterstock: 9, 25, 26t, 41, 49, 57, 58, 60t, 60b, 65, 68, 87, 93, 99, 124, 131,

Wellcome Collection: 74

Wikimedia Commons: 10t, 10b, 12, 14, 16, 17b, 18, 19, 20-1, 24, 28, 29, 30, 31t, 32, 33l, 37, 38, 42, 44, 45, 47, 50, 51, 52, 53, 54, 59, 63b, 73, 75, 76, 77, 79, 83, 84, 85, 86t, 88, 89, 92, 95, 97t, 98, 100, 101, 102, 103, 105bl, 105cl, 105r, 107, 108b, 110, 111, 112, 114, 115, 116, 119, 120, 121, 122, 123, 125, 126t, 127, 129, 130, 132, 133, 136, 137t, 137b, 138, 140, 141, 142, 144, 145, 147, 149, 150, 151, 152t, 152c, 152bl, 154, 156t, 157, 158, 159, 160, 161, 162, 163, 164t, 166, 167t, 167b, 168, 173t, 173b, 178, 180, 187l